COLLECTED POEMS

OTHER BOOKS BY
KENNETH BURKE

The White Oxen and Other Stories   1924
    Revised Edition *forthcoming*   1968

Counter-Statement   1931
    Revised Edition   1953
    Revised Edition *forthcoming*   1968

Towards A Better Life, A Series of Epistles, or Declamations   1932
    Revised Edition   1966

Permanence and Change, An Anatomy of Purpose   1935
    Revised Edition   1954
    Paperback Edition   1965

Attitudes Toward History   1937
    Revised Edition   1959
    Paperback Edition   1961

Philosophy of Literary Form, Studies in Symbolic Action   1941
    Paperback Edition (Abridged)   1957
    Revised Edition   1967

A Grammar of Motives   1945
    Paperback Edition   1962

A Rhetoric of Motives   1950
    Paperback Edition   1962

Book of Moments, Poems 1915–1954   1955

The Rhetoric of Religion: Studies in Logology   1961

Language As Symbolic Action: Essays on Life,
    Literature, and Method   1966

Perspectives by Incongruity,
    Edited by S. E. Hyman and B. Karmiller   1965

Terms for Order,
    Edited by S. E. Hyman and B. Karmiller   1965

Collected Poems,
1915 -1967
by
Kenneth Burke

Our moods do not believe in each other.
—Emerson

UNIVERSITY OF CALIFORNIA PRESS
Berkeley and Los Angeles / 1968

University of California Press
Berkeley and Los Angeles, California

Cambridge University Press
London, England

TO LIBBIE

FOREWORD TO BOOK OF MOMENTS

Lyrics are "moments" insofar as they pause to sum up a motive. They are designed to express and evoke a unified attitude towards some situation more or less explicitly implied.

In one's moments, one is absolute. Though there may not be current names for some of them, all moments are as though capitalized: Delight, Promise, Victory, Regret, Apprehension, Arrival, Crossing, Departure, Loneliness, Sorrow, Despair, etc. In summing up a past, they ambiguously contain a not yet unfolded future (in fact, a future that may forever remain in the state of sheer implication, as with the remote possibilities for good or evil that jurists have to consider, when speculating about the constitutionality of a new law).

Ideally, perhaps, one should break down a motive into many different kinds of moment. For instance, a poet might make it a rule that whatever he happened to vilify in one lyric, he would glorify in another, that whatever he wept about this time he would laugh about the next, etc. The ideal lyrist would probably speak through as many shifting personalities as the ideal dramatist.

But in practice, regardless of the many moods a person experiences in a day, only some of them lend themselves to his particular ways of expression. He skimps on the multiplication and diversification of moments, if only through inability to do otherwise.

Day after day, year after year, he may have a fairly fixed attitude towards something, and may in fact build the whole logic of his life in accordance with this attitude—yet of a sudden, for a spell, he may be invaded by some quite different attitude, and this irruption may be the element that, for him, falls into the pattern of a momentary poem.

Some of the past moments, here recovered from my records of dead selves (a selection extending back as far as adolescence) are *doctrinal* ("propagandistic," "didactic"). A poem is no less moody, through having turned from sensibility to ideation, though current literary views often conceal this fact. Ironically, much of the modern resistance to the *didactic* has been established through the influence of poets who themselves are *teachers.* But since they earn their living by didacticism, while their own verse-writing is done after hours, during vacations, or at whatever other time is felt to be decidedly *not* the classroom, they impose this imperious but naïve pattern of their lives upon their theory of poetry. Ideally, here again, the complete lyrist would not shun the didactic; he would love ideas at least as strongly as sensations, and preferably more; but he would range among them "moodily," and would never proffer a candidate for canonization without also attempting to write as good a brief as possible for the *advocatus diaboli.* Only by a maximum of such free ranging could poetry best help to keep us free.

Fortunately, some of the writer's more apprehensive moments have already been "disproved," except insofar as no moment can be disproved (since it will forever go on having been exactly what it was, thereby possessing at least a sheerly *grammatical* kind of "perfection").

As for the arrangement of these pieces:

Though it would certainly not be worth while trying to get them in their exact chronological order, their general trend is in that direction. The book opens with late items, puts in the middle some survivals from the Thirties, and ends on early work (the last three being sheer juvenilia, done in 1915-16). Then, in an appendix, a few items of prose are added (the "First Exercise" because it was meant to be "poetic" in an oratorical sort of way; the "Project for a Poem on Roosevelt" because this uncrystallized "pre-moment" might have some value as an indicator, helping to refresh our memories about the moods of those days, and thus to correct some of the unfairness that has since arisen with regard to them; the "Second Exercise" because there was a first, and because of a desire to round things out). Then, having let down the bars, we added a few prose epigrams ("Flowerishes"), since that form also is a variant of the "momentarily summarizing." The tune for the Imitation Spiritual "One Light in a Dark Valley," is included since it suggested itself along with the words.

Some of these pieces have previously been published, though most of the magazines in which they appeared have vanished. The list comprises: *Contact, The Dial, Furioso, The Hopkins Review, The New Masses, The New Republic, Rocky Mountain Review, Secession, Silo, The University Review*. Two are reprinted from an early book of short stories, *The White Oxen*. Many of the Flowerishes are reprinted from Hermes Scrolls.

K. B.

ACKNOWLEDGMENTS

As regards the later sections of this book, I hereby gratefully acknowledge my indebtedness to those editors who printed some of these pieces in their publications.

From *Poetry* I here reprint: "A Letter From the Center," "Here and Now," "To the Memory of e. e. cummings," "And Here I Am, Fighting Dandelions," "Heavy, Heavy—What Hangs Over," and "An Assertion to End On."

From *The Nation:* "The Poet, on His Grand Climacteric," "Civil Defense," "Caesar's Wife," "Big Claus and Little Claus," "A Citizen Looks at the Female Figures on an Ancient Jar," and "He Was a Sincere, etc." The "Lines Anent an Inquiry" was published in the Correspondence Columns.

From *The Kenyon Review:* "Poetic Exercise on the Subject of Disgruntlement," and "Verses From Among Prose."

From *Limbo:* "Case History," and "On Creative Dying: An Exercise."

From *Portfolio and Art News Annual:* "Recitation, for James Durante, Esq."

From *The Psychoanalytic Review:* "Prayer of the Newspaper Editor" (included in an essay, "The Thinking of the Body," which was reprinted in my *Language as Symbolic Action*).

From *Pittsburgh Festival* and *The Hudson Review:* "Old Nursery Jingle Brought up to Date." It was also published in *Language as Symbolic Action*.

From *The Journal of General Education:* "Didactic Avowal" (there entitled "A Confession, Didactically").

From *The Centennial Review:* "As the Curtain Rises."

From *The New York Review of Books:* "The Early Hour" (translation of a poem by Hermann Hesse).

From *The Kenyon Collegian* (a supplement, *A Tribute From the Community of Letters* to John Crowe Ransom): "Dawn in Autumn in Vermont."

From *Stand:* "At Yosemite."

From *Saturday Review:* "On Putting Things in Order."

From *Location:* the titular poem, "Introduction to What."

The poem "Ejaculations Anent a Flaming Catastrophe" was printed in my *Language as Symbolic Action.*

And I wish to thank Harcourt, Brace & World, Inc., for permission to include quotations from E. E. Cummings' *One Hundred Selected Poems,* in my lines to his memory.

K. B.

BOOK OF MOMENTS
Poems 1915–1954

INTRODUCTION TO WHAT
Poems 1955–1967

IN CONCLUSION

BOOK OF MOMENTS
Poems 1915–1954

PROBLEM OF MOMENTS

I knew a man who would be wonder-wise,
Having been born with both myopic eyes
Scratched in again.

"Than tyrannous moments, what more absolute,"
He asked, "except the motionless pursuit
Of us by pain?"

Note squirrel on log, how pert, now in, now out—
But classicists find either too much drought
Or too much rain.

(Wise, eyes, again
Absolute, pursuit, pain
Out, drought, rain)

8/22/54

Crowd in, my thoughts—we must be towards love.
See lo! the sun-up.
It's good to lull a bit o' bye.

(Don't take the stairs too fast, Gramp old boy.
Remember that pain a little left of centre—
How it leaves you one whole breath behind,
And in all the whole wide world there's not one
    idea good enough to pull you out again)

Death, I'm sure-fire yours in the long run

Don't crowd me, Death

CREATION MYTH

In the beginning, there was universal Nothing.
Then Nothing said No to itself and thereby begat
        Something,
Which called itself Yes.

Then No and Yes, cohabiting, begat Maybe.
Next all three, in a ménage à trois, begat Guilt.

And Guilt was of many names:
Mine, Thine, Yours, Ours, His, Hers, Its, Theirs—
        and Order.

In time things so came to pass
That two of its names, Guilt and Order,
Honoring their great progenitors, Yes, No, and Maybe,
Begat History.

Finally, History fell a-dreaming
And dreamed about Language—

(And that brings us to critics-who-write-critiques-of-
        critical-criticism.)

THE MOMENTARY, MIGRATORY SYMPTOM

I went to see a doc about a pain
That came and went and then came back again.

I wanted him to help me track it down
With every verb and adjective and noun.

We chased it in one ear and out the other,
And back and forth between my Dad and Mother.

Through liver, kidney, foot;
It never would stay put.

We chased it all around my neck and head
(With his great art)
How it would dart
Through chest and heart
Whenever I lay sleepless in my bed.

One moment here, one moment there,
As migratory as the air,
As fleeting as the breeze
Was this disease.

Now dull, then sharp; now quick, then lingering—
It was the damnedest thing.

When he was ready for his final say
And I was reaching for my purse to pay,

"All through your life," he said, "You'll have this trouble"—
And charged me double.

"If you would live as long as people can
Then simply die a very ancient man.

"This much at least about your aches is true:
If they last long enough, then so will you."

NEO-HIPPOCRATIC OATH

I swear by Apollo
whose temple was the navel of the world,
and by Æsculapius
the personalized first-principle of cure,
and by Hygiea
who taught the dirt of hygiene,
and by Panacea
though death is the only one cure for everything...
by all divinely summarizing terms, in fact,
I swear,
asking to be judged by their genius.
I will do as well as method shows me how.

Those who taught me
I'll make into parent-substitutes—
and if they are in need
I'll join in raising funds for them.

I would even teach my own sons
if such a thing were possible.

I would ply with wearisome advice
all persons who are bound to me
by unwritten contract
and the medicaments of custom.
I'll try to show when ills might be outwitted
by devilishly morbid ingenuity.

If any ask me help him die
I'll plead:
"Wait a little longer," and after that,
"Just a little longer," and so on
delaying the lethal dose as long as possible;
nor will I favor such mean misuse of healing
as makes men sick.

To no woman will I give a deadening device
designed to keep her from conceiving
bright new thoughts.

I will live a life of guilt-laden properness,
and though I cannot offer cures for stony hearts
I'll try not to demean
the work of those who would.

Wherever I go, I'll go asseverating for love of the art
and not to the ends of malice or sheerly venereal
        appetite.
And if I come upon unsavory private matters
I'll keep them to myself
except insofar as I noise them abroad to everyone
as observations about everyone.

If I live by these rules
may I deservedly prosper.
But if I break the rules
may any good that comes to me
come undeserved.

STAR-FIRE

I

When Morn-fire,
I in dew
Joy-swill

Say first
Not know just why, what.

Holla! Greet Morn-fire.
"Tinkle, tinkle, Morn-fire!"

Dew-full grapes
Not yet heavy-hang, but in dew.

Fly-things sing-sit
On grow-things.
Grow-things fly-sing.
Air light-bright.
"Tinkle, tinkle, Morn-fire!"

(Not sing-sit just—
But while sit, go-up almost.)

I in dew
Joy-swill
While Morn-fire.

First holla   last hello.
Each hello-holla
When first done all done.
Halló-la hélla-ló!

II

Noon-fire lead, fight
Lay foe
Lay womb-man.

Late-fire
Old Think-Stink.   (Brave one, no fear bunny.)

Morn-fire
Just kid.

"Tinkle, tinkle, Morn-fire!"
"Stinkle, stinkle, Think-fire!"
"Crinkle, crinkle, Lay-Fire!"   (Not Late-Fire!)

Wait.
Star-fire twinkle

Through dark.

TWO CONCEITS, ANENT LOVE

(A friend had written: "I enjoyed your analytical comments on Death. But a more difficult assignment would be a treatment of Love." Whereupon, some lines suggested themselves.)

I

Dear Love, whose plenties, were they all!
Forgive us, Love, should we by politics
Be too much troubled.

Knowing there is none other than this one,
If love enough,
Then men could need get less,
Yielding their holdings,
Giving up their killings.

Dear Love,

Not stars, not Hell, nor intermediate Earth,
But just,

Dear Love...

II

Surprise me, Love, by such quick presence
As if, were I walking in the woods,
Then looking about me, as if I raised my eyes
And—why—there suddenly you!   (and none other)

O Lovely Spirit of Nothing, given warm substance,
Born of Brightness,
Or of a lingering glance
Or a touch too prolonged but slightly
(No! born of Universal Empire!)
Surprise me, Love . . .

I'll say hello-goodbye,
In any way love-worthy.
Go! freshen some odd fellow's sheets
(Maybe my son's)
Or, more exactly, grace them with body-odors.

But let us wordy ones
Sing at your wedding
(as at a wake?)
And kiss you there.

NURSERY RHYME

(A Jingle for Mother Goosey)

Young Mrs. Snooks was sick of sex
But Mr. Snooks was soaked in it.

Wherever he beheld a hole
He took a stick and poked in it.

He even tried to frig a frog
But fell in the pond and croaked in it.

INCIPIENTLY, BY THE SEA

Dozing, he forgot his whereabouts
Then lo! awaking to the cosmic roar
Of the sea
(The onrushing, perpetual sea)

He never saw the sea
So jammed with water

ALKY, ME LOVE

Spirit of Alcohol,
Bejeez,
One by one we have failed you.

Jack's liver, Tom's kidneys,
Bill's pump, Howard's bean
(they took him off in a wagon)—
Always there was something or other
Just couldn't stand it.

Here's the roster:
Ulcers, high blood pressure, cyanosis,
obesity, diabetes, insomnia, the shakes—
And other such.

Herb's arteries held out,
But his money couldn't.
That night he told off his boss,
It all seemed so simple at the time.
What a load was lifted from his mind,
But the next day, oof!

Alky, me Love,
We have been unworthy of you,
With our pills and dieting and resolves and
       going slow.

It's a dreary outfit we've come to be,
We, the Dispirited.
Everything is one long morning-after.
(We were the real thing in our day, though)

Well, damn it all:
Down the hatch, old man . . .
Bottoms up, old girl . . .
Here's to you—

AN OLD LIBERAL LOOKS TO THE NEW YEAR, 1953

A friend had written, saying: "God, what a fantastic situation, when activities legal in 1935 lead to one's being regarded as a criminal in 1952." We pondered on his observation, thus:

> Now things are getting turned around,
> As turned around as things can be.
> And the social conscience of '35
> Becomes the treason of '53.
>
> What you did then, all virtuous and legal,
> Is now adjudged a crime against the Eagle.
>
> You said, "It's coats we need, both new and old,
> To keep us warm in the financial cold."
> I think you'd better plead that you did not,
> Now that the weather has become so hot.
>
> Be suppliant,
> Recant.
>
> You said, "Let's help Democracy in Spain."
> Well, lad, I think you'd better say again.
> Such attitudes are now deemed vile and ranko,
> To be quite Franco.
>
> You said, "Let us protect the immigrant."
> Recant.
> You would defend our foreign-born?
> Unblow your horn.

Were you adaptive during the depression?
You're now a captive, with or sans confession.
The situation then?   Forget it, brother.
The situation has become another.

What then was good is now proclaimed polluted,
So let the Newer Freedom be saluted.

Did you occasionally rant,
Finding in talk a stimulant?
Were you a bit too protestant?
Or not enough intolerant?
In social views vociferant?
In manifestoes jubilant?
In sponsorship insouciant?
Were you a parlor-pinkish termagant
Who liked with Charlie Marx to gallivant?

Recant!   Recant!
What you did then, to be elect,
Is now a crime in retrospect.

The realm of charity grows scant.
Recant.

STOUT AFFIRMATION

Whomsoever there are—
Whether enemies, than which there is several,
Or friends, than which there is few—
Hear me of what I am speak of,
Leaving me promulge.

A great amt. of beauties emplenish the world,
Wherein I would o'erglance upon.
There are those which you go out and exclaim:
"Why!   How brim-brim!"

I shall be concerning sank ships
Throughout the entire Endure-Myself,
And may my foes become stumbled.
But I want you should, my dear, transpire—
Always transpire, grace-full thanlike one.

You, most prettier sing-rabbit,
And by never,
And lessermost from beneath not—
Prith, give on't.

YES ! ! !

SONNET—TO CALIFORNIA

Now see how all our tribe
Growing excessive
Aims to be exemplary
In the ways of churchdom

Drunk, he skimmed off all the surface rocks
Bowled them into the bushes
To give the knoll
An air of classic calm,

Shouting "Classic calm—classic calm"
Making much noise in the name of silence
Like those that fight wars
In the name of peace.

Arise, Temples, somehow—
He is an old man among new mountains.

IDYLL, WITH INTERRUPTIONS

O California, o'er thy breasty knolls
I wander like a herd of cattle grazing.
But lest I fall into a fit of lazing
Behold a kindly bank of fog unrolls.

O California, o'er thy knoll-like breasts
I wander like a grazing herd of cattle,
Here finding all at peace except such battle
As gracious hostess wages with her guests.

O California, noble travelogue
Half endless vistas, half unending smog.

LINES IN THE SPIRIT OF NEGATIVE THEOLOGY

(conceived on a Peak south of San Francisco)

Wondrous One
Hail to Thee
In thy Thou-ness.

Thy vast hurled-forth void
Remotely peopled
Is from here sighted
As I lurk-look from Look-Out

Across the wide deep sweep
Of Ultimate No.

Like mountain-men
Peering at valley-people,
So then spoke I,
A valley-person.

ARCHAI

(in sleep, are you extended corpselike?
or crouching like a fœtus?
Do you sleep in tomb or womb?)

At night, insomniac,
Like menstruous woman huddled—
Our Hero to himself thinking:

"Head down, fœtus, gazing
Into self-pool of black night.
Like savant bending over microbes;
Or as if straining into eye of telescope,
To find there, reflected, a-glitter,
(one's own?) the star-face."

(do you, by prayers, give yourself over?
yield into sleep?
What rites lead out of stony vigil?)

Hear the Monster Insomniac
Thrashing and Tossing in his Bed.
Father Nembutal, teach him to sleep—
This Macbeth-hath-murdered-sleep,
This stabber of what royal guest?
Fore-guilty . . . king-killer.

(do you, imagining motions,
feel the eyeballs rub against closed lids?)

Let him write a Letter to the Institutionalized;
To the Prisoner in Solitary;
To the Horned Toad in a Cornerstone;
Saying:

"*Mea culpa, mea maxima culpa*—
And to you, nameless in solitary,
Deep in darkness,
Beating without power...
Salute!"

Salute to the air-voyage of Anti-Faust. He had said:
"No flight! I will each year dig down deeper."

Salute to the Poet
Who Saw the Sky
In a Puddle Under a Horse.

And what of Thersites,
Despised of all his tribe
(Whipped by power, wisdom, and heroic love, all three:
By Agamemnon, Ulysses, and Achilles),
Loathed by the bard that made him,
Ultimate filth, speaking against epic war?
What of Thersites?

Salute—
To Saint Thersites.

MERCY KILLING

Faithfully
We had covered the nasturtiums
Keeping them beyond
Their season

Until, farewell-minded,
Thinking of age and ailments,
And noting their lack of lustre,
I said:

"They want to die;
We should let the flowers die."

That night
With a biting clear full moon
They lay exposed.

In the morning,
Still shaded
While the sun's line
Crawled towards them from the northwest,
Under a skin of ice
They were at peace.

THE CONSPIRATORS

Beyond earshot of others, furtively,
He whispered, "You best"; she, "You above all."
It was a deal. They did conspire together,
Using the legalities, planning for preferment.

Going into the market, they got tables,
Chairs, and other properties from the public
Stock-pile, taking absolute possession
For them alone. These things, all no one else's,
They thought, plotting further to increase
Their store. To have, to hold, to love—theirs only.

And after dark, behind drawn blinds, with doors locked,
And lights off, wordless in wedded privacy,
They went and got out the family jewels,
Put his and hers together, playing treasure.

TRICK WEATHER

Snow-bearing wind
Among dried leaves
On oak saplings
Sizzles like spring rain
This February late afternoon.

Soon leaves fall, scatter
In March wind.

Oak leaves blowing in March
Sure sign of spring

NIGHT PIECE

O pulsant autumnal jungle
Restore me to thy rhythm
Teach me the knack.

I have stood on the edge of the jumping-off place
Waiting.

Have looked down
To see still stars at the bottom of a lake;
Looked out
Upon dark riddle within.

O mad dreaming absolute City
O Nature's Babylon
Make me   of thy rhythm
Make me   of thy pageantry.

PART OF A LETTER

Remember that night, after the card game
We went bumping down the road
drunk
insulting each other.

You said things so vicious
the next day you apologized.

But I could not recall a one of them.
I was robbed.

Yours for that most momentous of words: "Vindication"—
it is the labyrinthine word.
All hail to Mighty Æschylus.

Beat the devil, beat the devil, beat the devil,
Beat the devil, beat the devil, beat the...

(Hear the train
Drive steadily on
Towards nowhere)

COMPLIMENT, IN PASSING

What rustling went through the dry leaves?
Was it some little animal?
Or whisp of wind?

What darkling moment went by?

A little mincing skunk, perhaps?
If so, he understands; he won't act meanly—
Not like the headlines.

I'll set no trap for you, odd fellow,
Nature's gentleman,
So given to withholding—

INVECTIVE AND PRAYER

Were everybody to spit in the ocean at once
It would make little difference.
                              Hence our hero,
Though sicklied o'er with the pale thought of caste
And ailing physically, found no good ground
For public bellyaching.

                              Assailed by radio
Booping vug-music for brigs and gunds to neg by,
He said: It stinniks.
                         Noting the maggot-ripe
Indoctrinaysh towards greater global frenzy,
He but felt a dull pain in the pain-receiver.
                                          Confronting
Professional pronouncements, he glumly edsay itshay.

(Sweetness, of the softly yielding hair,
You are mirác, you are entránce, terríf.
This little piggy must be brought to market.)

He knew the country was so stinko rich,
The rest of the world would sit up all night trying
To keep our politicos from making monkeys of themselves.
He knew there was less religion in a carload of cigarettes
Than in the Bishop Spookler's spiritual mug.
He watched the superguns and blasts that beckoned:

"Come, Killers, Here's to Blow the World Apart."
And he wondered: Would they pick a pissant for president?

    Dear God, if God there be,
    Please welcome me.

    (Far from the noise
    Of Michigan's Detroise.

    Make me as mild
    As a little child.)

    In the deep
    Of Thy Sleep.

AUTUMNAL DAY IN AUGUST

So?
Like the fall
He roves?

Startled, through a rip in his shirt,
To feel his own skin
Still smooth?

Alone is he?

Ready for what may be next—
Like birds flocking to make a big whirr?

Not off, surely,
For the Ultimate South?

(Not until it doesn't matter)

FAUSTKUNDE

Wenn ein Mensch in seinem Bette liegt,
So denkt er an sehr fürchterliche Dinge;
Fragt sich, ob grosses Unglück ihn umbringe,
Während in den Wogen der Ewigkeit er wiegt.

Wenn ein Mensch auf seinen Füssen steht,
So denkt er an fast irgend etwas nicht.
Lächelnd nennt er sich einen Bösewicht,
Während Galgenweg entlang er fröhlich geht.

Was mich betrifft: Seitdem ich älter bin,
Beim Sitzen denk' ich, wie in Jugendtagen
Mit grossem Jammer und viel Unbehagen
Ich Faust's Faust war, die eigene Verführerin.

TEMPORARY WELLBEING

The pond is plenteous
The land is lush,
And having turned off the news
I am for the moment mellow.

With my book in one hand
And my drink in the other
What more could I want

But fame,
Better health,
And ten million dollars?

ALCOHOLIC LION

I was once a believer,
But I am that no more,
Since they took me to the jungle-land
Where I heard the lion roar.

What does the lion roar with?
His head, or tail, or feet?
Or does he roar all over
When he would have his meat?

He stands outside his cavern,
To roar the whole world down.
And he roars in many a tavern
When he gets loose in town.

PYRE

"Make of me black smoke," cried Æschylus,
"Mounting to Heaven."

And I saw storage tanks ablaze, waves rich black
Boiling hurriedly upward.

Near the ground, a violent crackle-clamor;
Above that, softly, an inrush of air;
Higher, the slow drifting into nothing.

DIALECTICIAN'S PRAYER

Hail to Thee, Logos,
Thou Vast Almighty Title,
In Whose name we conjure—
Our acts the partial representatives
Of Thy whole act.

May we be Thy delegates
In parliament assembled.
Parts of Thy wholeness.
And in our conflicts
Correcting one another.
By study of our errors
Gaining Revelation.

May we give true voice
To the statements of Thy creatures.
May our spoken words speak for them,
With accuracy,
That we know precisely their rejoinders
To our utterances,
And so may correct our utterances
In the light of those rejoinders.

Thus may we help Thine objects
To say their say—
Not suppressing by dictatorial lie,
Not giving false reports
That misrepresent their saying.

If the soil is carried off by flood,
May we help the soil to say so.
If our ways of living
Violate the needs of nerve and muscle,
May we find speech for nerve and muscle,
To frame objections
Whereat we, listening,
Can remake our habits.
May we not bear false witness to ourselves
About our neighbors,
Prophesying falsely
Why they did as they did.

May we compete with one another,
To speak for Thy Creation with more justice—
Coöperating in this competition
Until our naming
Gives voice correctly,
And how things are
And how we say things are
Are one.

Let the Word be dialectic with the Way—
Whichever the print
The other the imprint.

Above the single speeches
Of things,
Of animals,

Of people,
Erecting a speech-of-speeches—
And above this
A Speech-of-speech-of-speeches,
And so on,
Comprehensively,
Until all is headed
In Thy Vast Almighty Title,
Containing implicitly
What in Thy work is drawn out explicitly—
In its plenitude.

And may we have neither the mania of the One
Nor the delirium of the Many—
But both the Union and the Diversity—
The Title and the manifold details that arise
As that Title is restated
In the narrative of History.
Not forgetting that the Title represents the story's Sequence,
And that the Sequence represents the Power entitled.

For us
Thy name a Great Synecdoche
Thy works a Grand Tautology.

BLOOD ON THE MOON

(On the Occasion of a Total Lunar Eclipse,
December 1945)

Last night I saw blood on the moon.

Disposed about
This one surly marvel the stars, intent,
Stood out
Aghast—

Stared like at an accident.

Last night, with the moon blood-dull,
I thought how I'd seen as a child
The crushed skull
Of a man new killed.

Strange,
That this ever-changing
Principle of a girl's changes
Itself so rare shows blood, and now strikes me
With an old memory.

There's the virgin for a man to take last:
Piercing the maidenhood of his own walled past.

THE WRENS

The wrens are back!

Their liquid song, pouring across the lawn—
(Or, if the sunlight pours, the wren's song glitters)
Up from the porch,
                    Into the bedroom, where
It is the play of light across a pond,
Sounding as small waves look: new copper coins
Between the seer and the sun.

                    Herewith
Is made a contract binding the brightly waked
Sleeper and his wren, neither the wren's
Nor his, but differently owned by both.

Behind the giving-forth, wren history;
Man-history behind the taking-in.

(Mark the city as a place where no
Wrens sing, as though April were seas of sand,
With spring not the burial of lilac,
                    but heat quaking above stone.)

                              After magnetic storms
Had made all men uneasy, but those the most
That feared the loss of salary or love,

The wrens are back!

THOUGHTS ON WAR

They are getting ready very fast
already they are preparing themselves
by secretly knowing that the wars cannot satisfy

now they must all get ready in the same way
paying one another to pull the strings of one another

huddled together
among the clutter of perfect machinery,
not knowing what to fight for
they will be systematic
and fight with twice the efficiency
or will be sullen
and fight with twice the vengeance

what we work to build
is what we become
what then can we become
if we work to build machines that blast
or to build the routines that run the machines?
not scenes for wise acts

if weak in love
we will be powerful with the engines of destruction

or there must be a great commingling of persons
lest there be a great over-running of hordes
—there must be much going in and out of one another,
otherwise they will smash a man
as though he were the house of an enemy
and they outside it.

they grow angry,
looking exaltedly for victims—
and Raw New Money.

what they have lost in the street
let them look for in the wood path

it is not in the engine, but in bodies

is it lost in the bursting bomb?
it may be found again
in the bursting blossom

ENIGMA

I love you as a stranded ship the beach
Where a dead body glistens on the shore.
And while the moonlight gives a form to each,
I hear the formless jungle's distant roar.

My thoughts of you are like the nameless clutter
Of wavelets twinkling on the ocean's tide;
Ten thousand dumb for every one I utter—
Dumb as this drowned man lying on his side.

The cliff that rises by the water's edge—
Were I there, looking down upon the sea,
I could not know, on peering from its ledge,
Whether the body was my love, or me.

SOCIAL ARITHMETIC

If they give us five,
We shall but ask for ten.
If they give us two,
We shall but ask for four.
But should they give us nothing, then
We'll ask for all the world, and more.

SOCIAL GEOMETRY

In is not out,
And out is not in;
But this much is certain:
It's bad luck to win.

FRIGATE JONES, THE PUSSYFOOTER

Frigate Jones was very slow and fat,
In fact, he was the perfect bureaucrat.

With hands like feet, and feet in turn like legs,
It was his job to lightly step on eggs.

He watched the scene as gamblers watch the ticker,
And bought or sold upon the slightest flicker.

For he could read the weather in the sky,
And in the name of mankind, fed his "I."

He never found it hard to speak the truth,
Since he believed as he was told, forsooth.

At pussyfooting he was Number One,
And in this gentle way his race was run.

But give him rope enough, and I opine
He'll hang himself upon a party line.

LULLABY—FOR ONESELF AS ADULT MALE

O'er soft the gentling soft you smoothly on—
In bringing   in compliance   to away—
The go,   the going,   ought-to-go,   and gone
                    Give us
Forgive   this unforgiving day.

The undulance from objects into mind
Yes   no   yes   no   of patient
              Tick   (death)   tock.
Here is the past and future intertwined—
Each man the key,   and everything the lock.

Child of the centuries, sleep.
Sweet bearded darling, sleep.

OFFERING FOR THE TIME CAPSULE

On those who burn parliaments, and books, and treaties

Know there was a moment came and went,
When what some said and what the others said,
When both were found to be incompetent
And we dared hope that there might rise instead

A gentler doctrine, lacking the haste of these,
That would, in meeting matters of the State,
Have made us see things as the gardener sees—
This doctrine came—but fraily, and too late.

Arose the Teutons yapping with belief
That made their minds the replica of fists
And gave heroic, ominous relief
After the scorn of France's theorists.

It was their best they drew on for their worst—
It was the nation's greatness that did fall—
They were by mental benefits accursed,
And in their madness, metaphysical.

Know that the time when jungle strife was through
And there was bounty here for everyone,
Know that precisely then the contest grew
And what the books had done was now undone.

Know that we caught the fleeting glimpse of peace—
Know that we saw the mildly glowing light
Of ways that could have given us release—
And then we sank into a dreary night.

INDUSTRIALIST'S PRAYER

Lord, make all men feel that they are suffering from the lack
of my commodity. Let them not *really* need it, since
I would be uncharitable in asking that. Let them
just *think* they need it—and let them think so, very
very hard. And let them get the money somehow to
buy it.

Not from the government, since that would increase my
taxes. Not from higher wages, since that would
increase my costs of production. And not as manna
from Heaven, since that would cause inflation.

All that I ask of Thee—Lord—is just one more miracle, that
good business shall not perish from the earth.

ONE LIGHT IN A DARK VALLEY
Imitation Spiritual

One light in a dark valley
   and the mist is falling like rain
One light in a dark valley
   and I'm alone again.

One light in a dark valley
   and I am all alone.
One light in a dark valley
   is all I can call my own.

One light in a dark valley
   and the darkness movin' about.
One light in a dark valley
   and now that light has gone out.

No light in a dark valley
   nothin' but darkness and me.
No light in a dark valley
   for all eternity.

Oh . . .

Light it up Lord, make it shine, good
God'll make his heaven bright(i)ly mine.
I'll look through every window and I'll walk through every
   door
And there'll be such gladness 'round me I won't want for
   any more.

UNEASY THOUGHT OF PEACE

In our street
We lie late in bed
On dull winter mornings
And think of the dead.

In our street
We lie in our hovels
And hear it having snowed
By the scraping of shovels.

BUILDINGS SHOULD NOT BE TALL

Buildings should not be tall, that we be spared
The need to walk in gulches.   Of their pride
We are the squalor. We the traffick-eyed,
Stench-nostriled, Klaxon-eared and thinning-haired,
Inhabiting a city's underside,
By this man-made biology prepared
To cower in meekness, hurried and beglared,
And somehow live until we've somehow died.

These are our masters, basking in the sun—
It is our owners that we crawl among.
In such granitic utterance they reveal
Self-portraitures of greed that rose up, when
A grasping brood expressed in stone and steel
Its detestation of its fellow-men.

FOR A MODERNIST SERMON

You'll have an eight-cylinder car in heaven—
Air conditioning—
Indirect lighting—
a tile bathroom and a white porcelain kitchen.

Despite the phenomenal growth of population,
there'll be no traffic problem,
if you would drive out
to the Garden of Eden
for a week-end.

O the celestial sundaes—
all flavors made with the purest chemicals.

No strike—no speed-up—no lay-off—
everybody a coupon-clipper in heaven,
living in peace, on the eternal drudgery
of the damned.

All will be fragrant and quiet in heaven,
like the best real estate in Westchester.
All noise and stench segregated
to the under side of the railroad.

In heaven,
When you want something,
you just fill out an order
and your want is met like magic,
from the Power-plants
　　Assembly rooms
　　　Factories
　　　　Presses
　　　　　Forges
　　　　　　Mines
　　　　　　　Mills
　　　　　　　　Smelteries
　　　　　　　　　and Blast-Furnaces

　　of hell.

PLEA OF THE PEOPLE
(1933)

Hear us in our prejudices—
Listen to us in our special pleading—
who would choose warmth and chuckling,
But fear desolation.
World too earnest,
In which we cannot be without vast documents.
Great understanding is needed, if we are but to have shelter.
Burden of a State
Wherein, by merely waiting,
We put misery upon our fellows.

See: we are fists, teeth, and searching, calculating eyes—
We have the sharpness of tigers about to leap forward.
An armory of nerve and muscle.
We are all girded, by the power of hating.
By the Jungle we are fitted.
Our eyes burn out of dark corners.
Leave us but our bodies and our sufferings, and we are armed.

We are weeping—
There is softness and gentleness within us—
We would be men of goodwill,
Bringing gifts to one another.

To be strong in hate or to rot in wretchedness—
Do not force us to this choice that is no choice:
Broken, or needing vengeance.

Let us use our muscles and our minds in service.
With eye, hand, and mental keenness let us
Be busied for the good of many.
Permit us to have as brothers
Men whom if they are less than brothers
We must vilify and lynch.

We plead
That the prey and combat of the Jungle state may be abolished
—Into the air
All about us
From tenements, streets, parched marginal farms,
We plead for the right of gentleness.

Our victors are not happy.
Those above us, who must seek profit,
They cannot.
And so must threaten us,
Or imprison us,
Or hang us,
Or burn us in the chair of justice,
Or goad us to bewildered conflicts with one another.

We have even hoped for the trenches,
That men might again be cronies.
We have even told ourselves how by the wars
We might again be brought together,

By the helpfulness of slaughter.
The wars are fuller than the peace,
In fellowship.

There is within us a realm of loveliness,
A willingness of warmth and chuckling.
All that we are as men working together
Waits within us.
We plead that our State be made in its image,
That children may retain their exceptional sweetness.

Let us arise like music—
Many instruments,
Singing in different voices,
Varied designs and timbres,
Disparate rhythms,
One single symphony.
Let us be like one chord set vibrant,
To which others are also set vibrant.

No less can save us.
No less than the blaze of glory,
Our vast uniting.

ATLANTIS

There was an island of Antiquity—
Well favored with an equatorial sky—
Where Babylonic galleys used to lie
And inland music sounded cumbrously.

Though long accustomed to such clemency
It felt obscure disturbances, whereby
Emitting a huge geologic sigh
It lurched, and gently sank beneath the sea.

Its marbles now, in pale aquatic hues
Stand aimless, posturing on heavy floors
Where parchments waver, limp and yellowish
And houses front on darkened avenues
Bearded with sea-growth, promenades for fish
With mournful faces peering through the doors.

FROM OUTSIDE

(He mounts the stairs. And while pausing outside the door, he experiences motives like the riot of a witches' Sabbath, or like many insects throbbing.)

Passed through the tunnelled length of corridor,
Mounted the shaft of squarely winding stairs.
(With each new floor ascended he could peer
Down the dark well upon his increased absence,
While episodes of undistinguished sound
Grew into words or footsteps, purposes
Unseen, and after having been such, faded.)
Slowly, he said, I rise above the street—
Until he stood beneath the milky dawn
Of an internal, sunless, angled sky,
Stood there and waited, asking—should he knock.

"Open!" whined the Wheezy Wort,
"Open!" croaked the Donker Toad.
Crooked Broomstick, Snide, and Snort
Welcome me to this abode.

"Open!"noises everywhere,
Floor noise, sink noise, noise of breathing.
How my ears are seething
In this empty air.

Snide, Snort, Broomstick and all
Answer my silent call.

There stood waiting. . . . Had the general hum
Risen and fallen to a common pulse,
He could have called this place a bog, quaking
With life, made cheap by multitude, and nameless.

THEIR PREFERABLE WAYS

*(He thinks of gallantry under conditions whereby
silence could give consent.)*

Out of their casual speech and unsought meetings,
Out of much unintended deprecation,
Arose a day of subterfuge, a fiction
To bridge the distance of acquaintanceship.

Walking, they found it pleasant to assume
That she through blindness was in need of guidance,
And he might lead her with authority,
Piloting her to some familiar spot
Made new to them by being come upon
In such an unaccustomed manner. When
After their various ludicrous mistakes
They stumblingly arrived, she fell inert,
Less out of weariness than pedantry.

He altered his conceit: "Blind thing," he said,
"You are a bundle dropped among these woods.
Now, worse than blind: will-less, inanimate,
You lie upon this alien ground, a Bundle."

Musing aloud, he chose to speculate
Why such a bundle lay there, bringing forth
Gallant conjectures, dismissed gallantly.
"A madman left this Bundle; no one else,
Though under fright or planning to return,
Would risk this possibility of loss."

So logical a man would next enquire
What valuables the bundle might contain,
And from its rich appearance hope to find
"Such goods as in their way are sweet as the
Faint sound of distant revelry and music."

But how unloose this Bundle? Would it not
"Protect itself by wielding of a spell
Whereby, if I should venture to approach,
I should be struck down, palsied and afire?"

The game was graced by one more regulation,
Requiring that the bundle should convey
Some sign to him by manners known to bundles.
Did he but lightly touch the hair, no more,
Only the hair, and if the bundle gave
Consent, then let it stir itself in answer.

"It yields!   Observe the head at this
Slight pressure turning.   Miracle of nature—
That I am here.   A double miracle—
That I am here and Bundle should have spoken!"

THE METAPHOR OF JACK IN THE BANDBOX

(He thinks of outright lewdness, and of subsequent lewd jealousy.)

There is a little box, light to the touch,
Its sides and cover painted red and gold,
With shapes designed to entertain the eye,
But emblems once of blasphemy and magic.

The cover of this box is made secure
By a small catch of wire which, when released,
Permits the lid to open with a snap
And lo!—spring-driven, out pops a villainous head,
Thereat to wag and compliment and grin,
Parading his lewd presence here among us.

How would it constitute a breach of love,
Were one hour given to other arms?
It would not bring you reason to suspect
That even one small corner of her mind
Had been attacked by fester; that her smile,
Laid over you at parting, as the lock
Snapped into place behind you, ever froze
With treacherous imagery.   Not even while
The sluices of your blood first swelled and knocked,
Could you compound an anodyne of slander,
Unable through your memory of her sweetness,
To steel yourself against this loss by hating.

CONCLUSION

*(Turning away and leaving, he imagines people exalted in
the form of their own enormous shadows—and he ends on
the thought of sharing in the grandeur of books.)*

If I had more than visited—I came,
And fearing sufferance, crept away again;
Turned and went down the steps—and were the air
Some heavy, sluggish liquid thing in which
Our breathing takes on shape and color, I
Should have retraced the fog of my own coming,
With choice of any course I might prefer,
Free to take east or west or north or south,
Or any of the subtleties of such.

Here was a failing corner of myself,
Offered to you before the world and I
Had cut it from me—vestige of such doubts
As those must quell who, meeting fear, can say:
"Out fear—we are not paid to fear."

Now, lest the trumpet of the dawn blare forth
Unheeded, I affirmatively rise,
Whistle my dog, and make off up the hill—
Finding thereby some method to forget
What dismal mock-economy this is:
That in scant years out of eternity
One sees his nearest step to happiness
In contemplation of another's splendor.

Is there some vast and melancholy place
Where, as explorers in the Arctic sun
Behold huge transcripts of their bodies cast
In shadow on the clouds, perceiving there
Each move transmogrified into its own
Enormous replica, so we could find
The distant repetition of ourselves
In magnified comparison?

Such sudden region is the realm of art—
And as the day dissolves in nightfall, note
How we must enter shivering from the mist
And find the match by touch, and light the lamp,
And shed the silent downpour on the desk
To dissipate the evening's tyranny—
Affording that one thing which man has added:
The articulate, analytic sound.
Welcome! ... Here again. .... Here I am back—

HERE ARE THE FACTS

Here are the facts, given as I have known them:

Last night I slept with my shame bared to the ceiling;
The bed was hot against my back and buttocks;
My arms were swollen with the bites of black-flies.

And now the thunder-caps quit dropping below the horizon;
The thunder-caps are beginning to march above me;
I watch, with the salt stinging the rim of my eye-balls.

A breeze starts up, making the lake look blue-black;
The blue-black swallows fly even more click-jaggy;
The green trees in the distance become also blue-black.

I close the windows fronting on the southwest;
The thunder falls immediately on the lightning;
And the rush of rain in the trees upon the thunder.

The black-flies of Massachusetts are blown into New
        Hampshire;
And the black-flies of New Hampshire are blown into
        Maine, while
Those of Maine are blown, some into Canada and some into
        the ocean.

Water hits in bucket loads against the wood shed;
Water hurries beneath the dried up shingles;
Water drips mysteriously in the pantry.

The rain settles now to a steady business;
It lays itself without violence over the pastures;
Night falls, with the rain now gently piddling.

A new wind falls upon us from the northwest;
Veering, it whips the fog along the hillsides;
And shoves the entire storm out of my knowledge.

A haze of light spreads in the north horizon;
Pale shafts of light waver on the north horizon.
And puffs of light like dust wave toward the zenith.

A calm lies on the face of the earth and waters;
It sits among the trees and in the valleys;
A frost is nosing against the wild cherry blossoms.

The sun comes up as clean as a brand-new dollar;
The pink sun edges flatly above the skyline;
As rash as a blast of unexpected music.

Praise to the Three-God, Father, Son and Spirit;
Who, as He found Himself at the beginning;
So is He now, and so shall be forever!

VER RENATUS ORBIS EST

No, I shall not go and look out of the window;
A city of five million mucous excitements;
I know of a pond now in Ohio
　　Where before bed some students are sitting;
Spring! calling us to the major cycle of conception.

Timor mortis versus tædium vitæ;
Noises from a distance without clarified meaning;
Hot flesh massed dissatisfied in the movies
　　Accepting the used-up breath in silence;
Spring! calling us to the major cycle of conception.

Deep buried wombs growing restless;
Dark sperm pressing against its prison;
Halleluia!　let cathode and anode be united.

EROTICON: AS FROM THE GREEK ANTHOLOGY

Lamp, when there is a faint shuffling of sandals
        outside my door,
And the odor of unguents and perfumes
Calls me like a blare of trumpets, so that I
Arise hastily from my table ... go out, lamp.
For tonight I shall be laying aside my text
To become the grammarian of sweet Amyctis' body.

AS FROM A GREEK ANTHOLOGY

Do the violets, like me, tug at their roots this warm day of
        late autumn?
Already I can imagine late April, yet we have not even had
        our first snow-flurry.
When I was young, spring came upon me suddenly, with me
        still thinking of the pleasures of the sleigh.
But if I expect it always earlier and earlier
I shall soon overtake it by a cycle,
And be expecting spring in the springtime.

THREE SEASONS OF LOVE

When dirty snow softens the matted grass,
And Proserpina gathering up her garments
Prepares to return from the dull couch of Dis,
And the trees are busy with their fresh ornaments
In making beautiful her path to Olympus;
Then I love.
I am nobly desirous—
And as I seek my mate,
I keep one holy eye on Heaven.
Yet my love is that same thing
That perpetuates the snakes.

When the green leaves are no longer glistening,
And the sap in me and in the trees is sluggish,
And the world becomes a dangerous velvet,
A lazy warmth,
Then I love.
Then Heaven slinks away before the prurient
           'cellos wailing at my soul,
My love is that same thing
That rots great nations.

But when the chill leaps up,
And the leaves, with a beautiful melancholy
Get out their silks to die in,
Like great lifeless Vikings sent out upon the sea,
Majestic in their blazing, wealth-laden galleys;
Then I love—
Swimming in the moonlight

Racing in the cold
The prankish autumn moon
And a healthy shivering
Catch me up in rough hands,
Hands sooted with the black of roasted potatoes,
And trip me
And pummel me
And roll me over the hills.
My love is that same thing
That swilled new cider and danced in the barn.

THE MONSTER

As softly as the moon's rays on the floor—
The rays were broken by a gaunt, dark chair—
He stole in silence to her sleeping there,
Crept darkly through the shadow-buried door,

And dared one cautious kiss, nor nothing more,—
A scarce half-touching of her tousled hair;
As easily as when the summer air
Breathes on a flower, and dies of its rich store.

Then from her sleep escaped a little cry;
Her body trembled slightly though she slept;
The watcher caught a shiver of her eye

For through closed sleeping lids she saw a form
Approach her, while its breath stirred like a storm.
She saw it crouch; it dripped black blood, and crept.

RHAPSODY UNDER THE AUTUMN MOON

Dewy, perplexing, wide-eyed moon,
Tonight I suddenly awoke, and felt you—and your poem.
Here in my bed I understood the pagan moon.
With your Gothic savagery laughing at my furniture,
I understood you.

Far away I should be,
Out in the hollow forests,
Where you would chase me,
And paralyze me with eternities.
Out with the purring trees as they shiver and cuddle in your
        flannel light,

Wild, crazy, alone,
Where I could tipple on heedless myths of Dionysoi and
        Persephonæ,
And moonstruck, flee from satyrs and druids,
And rejoice in the melancholy pleasure of soughing with
        the leaves.

Those leaves! how would they look in the godless
        moonlight?
Those gorgeous corpses which in the sun are a red
        changeable silk
As they lie in state;
And which I have only seen huddled pell mell onto the back
        seats of tourists' automobiles,
As shamelessly as fanciful children driven into the school
        room.

Artemis!
Racing over the hermit hillsides,
And dampening the lakes in the valleys with your splendor,
You do not hunt only for bears and the deer.
Rather, you would sneak up to peep slyly at the quivering
        field mice,
Funny little old men, and as busy as their whiskers.
And then you would jump at them,
And send them scattering in a panic.

For you are so awesome
That you love to trifle,
And to think you are a little boy stepping on ants.
And you are the spirit of healthy destructiveness,
The spirit which charmed the Teuton torrents
Until they poured headlong over the marbles of Rome.

As you play upon the pumpkins that I hear are frosted in the
        autumn,
You scare up all the mischievous sprites that are in us,
And tickle them until they are wide awake, and eager for evil.

I should be wild, now, in the forest,
Sick with fear at your motionless, poisonous loneliness.
I should be torturing myself deliciously with inspired lies
        about a million grotesque deities.
Or perhaps, as you glisten at me through the chilly
        tombstone branches,
I should have with me quick nervous youths
Whose hearts beat too often;

Momentarily atavistic boys, pulsing with the excitement of
        the carnival—
Soft, breathless, cold-nosed girls, laughing and panting with
        the outlandishness of the Hallowe'en that's in them.
Then I could rave and tumble,
And do something daring,
Whether it be to steal a kiss,
Or to run away with a mountain.

Artemis! Artemis!
Let me dream hideous dreams about you,
And tell myself you are maddening me.
Let me build altars to you,
And elaborate dithyrambs to you,
And be mightily awed by you,
And rejoice when you have torn off every strip of your dark
        garments,
And appear before me, chaste and naked.
Drive me foaming among the weird bare trees I cannot name,
Until I am as desperate as the daughter of the river god
In flight to save her womb from the seed of Apollo.
Bewitch me!
Cast me back upon the rocks of Attica.
Let me worship you as violently as the violet-weaving
        Lesbian could worship Aphrodite.
Mystic moon,
I would *live* my rhapsody!

Dewy, perplexing, wide-eyed moon,
The traffic mumbles that you are not Artemis.

APPENDIX

PROJECT FOR A POEM ON ROOSEVELT

I. Era of gestation. Lineaments of a theory of *fame*. Roman rather than Christian notions of purpose. That is, *political* coördinates, as contrasted with *family* coördinates. Possessing at the start the insignia of family, he feels no great need to justify himself by the founding of a line. Possessing at the start the taste of wealth, he lacks the incentives towards the more naïve aspects of justification by business success. As with feudalists of the old South, a sense of sufficient family and sufficient wealth edges him towards *politics* as the fitting mode of social expression.

II. Critical interlude. His attack of paralysis. The resultant *physical necessity* of patience, since his cure cannot be hurried. Sense of *limitations* (how to work within limitations). Training in *vagueness*, resulting from the long interim (psychologically imposing) wherein there is a distinct breach between attitude and act. That is: The healthy man spontaneously coördinates mind and body; angry, he clenches his fist; elated, he throws back his shoulders and strides; affectionate, he embraces; wanting, he grasps. But here instead we get a long training in *dissociation* between the aim and the fulfilment. A slight expression must serve instead of the total and untrammeled expression. Hence, relativism. Theory of essence. That is: a slight act equals the full act *if it is in the spirit or direction of the full act.* In this he learns organically, through the trauma of illness, what Whitman and

William James learned (the thoroughness of illness teaches him what Whitman learned through the thoroughness of poetry, and James through the thoroughness of philosophy).

III. New approach. Picture of democracy as it works in business structure. Many conflicts among business interests. Not only conflicts between the hirers and the hired. Also internecine conflicts among the hirers, and internecine conflicts among the hired. How tariff may protect one hirer-hired group at the expense of another. How industrial centers as a whole can profit *for a time* at the expense of agrarian areas. How crooked promoters actually stimulate the speed-up of money (and hence the distribution of goods among all) until the false basis of their promises is disclosed. How wastage serves to promote the common good. Problem of *man as customer* (how can you sell to him, unless you give him the money to buy with?). Redistribution by taxation (redistribution in Rome; shift from land and corn to dole, money, as per soldiers' bonus). Political forms are the *dial on which all these conflicts register.* Every conflict in Congress reflects a conflict among business interests. How this condition affects political parties, whose "owners" (campaign donors) ask for more than party can give. (Insofar as a party acceeds, it ruins itself as an investment. "Party's first responsibility is to itself.")

IV. "Promise something to everybody, and mean it." ... "Let things shape themselves." ... "Be center of coördination." ... "Be the dissociation between the attitude and the act." ..."Be the resultant of conflicting forces." . . . "Wait and see." . . . "Send up brave words as trial balloons." . . . "Threaten—and make peace with the threatened."

V. Retrospect. View of critical moment, when he could have socialized banks. Too direct an act. Not in accordance with his number. Would have been an act out of character (neglectful of his trauma). Would have been *fame*, yes; but not *his* fame. [This section, we note, was to have been in first person!]

VI. The pulling and tugging goes on. A little of this, a little of that. "If they assert, and their assertions weigh against each other, be the pointer on the dial." The assertions of the moneyed interests are always written into the State (hence, in part, he respects their assertions, when he is seeking to guide their State). But the *conflict* of these assertions is already "between the lines" of their contracts. Hence, he will also read between the lines. No: he will *recognize* the man who does (but recognize him after his fashion, vaguely). That is: ambiguous encouragement to labor leaders. As a result:

VII. The new State emergent. The industrial union as one "estate." The large financial interests as another "estate." Economic reframing of political chambers. Financial grouping equals new "house of lords." Industrial union equals "house of commons." Old political institutions remain to muddle the symmetry.

VIII. Peroration. What the "lower house" will do for the "house of lords." Eventual extinction of latter as power. Has so happened before. "Let them love history more than their belongings."

"Write, then, a poem on the President." Admittedly, even a Lucretius would have had trouble making this project sing. And the last couple of stages do deteriorate greatly, even as a project. But these few lines serve at least to establish the mood, the underlying "moment":

                              Honor this man
         By bringing simple gifts, such bits of tin
         As, homeless under Hoover, derelicts
         Found among weeds, to make themselves a house.
         Our culture now is like those villages;
         It's knocked together, pulled from rubbish heaps,
         A church above a sewer. (What fitter place
         For Churches! Churches are worse than wasted if
         Erected on some spot that is itself
         A church. Build them upon our poverties,
         Nor let them, in their end, forget their source.)
         Let ties be kept unbroken. Let the low
         Bring fitting tributes, lowly ones.

FIRST EXERCISE FOR YEAR'S END

Like wires singing near a meadow, the new dawn rose, swelling silently towards full day, while tiny rivulets of light trickled with fragrance into all the nooks and crannies of the morning. Worms and little crushed insects began feeling glad in the bellies of birds. Insofar as was possible, darkness ceased pressing upon the surfaces of things. A soft motionless sliver of cloud was stretched in sharp suddenness across a slit in the otherwise uniform and brittle sky.

Already the Messenger was writing. Even in the pale dusk, he had begun—and he would still be at it when nature's rheostat of sunrise had been turned to full. He wrote:

Sir:

Since my last communication to you, Sir, new things have unfolded. Or at least, they seem to be unfolding. There are signs of some loss of faith in public promises, though the general sluggishness in the buying of baubles may indicate not so much a loss of faith in them as a drop in the means of testifying to such faith.

Some students (still no alarming number) have refused to be hazed in the normal manner. The churches are being stirred by an influx of new converts that bring turbulence and controversy into a realm heretofore quiescent. It was necessary that a certain impudent slave be put to death; having been commanded to fan the king, he was found to have added a secret contrivance whereby he also fanned himself. And it is rumored that there is unrest among the Lesbians, who are flocking about a stupendous Amazon-like Leader, or rather Leaderess, they call "Saint Lemming."

By now the petals of the day had almost fully opened. Indeed, some showed signs of loosening, as though they would drop before too many hours had been invisibly frozen in the warming sunlight. The Messenger continued:

In accordance with my instructions, Sir, I have sought for opportunities to meet people as it were by chance, addressing them as though confidentially, in the hopes that, by seeming to confide in them, I might bring them to confide in me, and thus to reveal whatever might be forming. Yet among wide ranges of the populace, there seems to be, rather, a race towards absolute nothingness. It is as though, to guard against the suspicion of dangerous thoughts, the people were learning to have no thoughts at all. And I find it very difficult to read the signs, when secrecy has become thus doubly self-protective, by not even letting itself know its own mind. But I do begin to glimpse a possible method, as in the case of the following incident:

Recently, in a public place, a weak and ineffectual fellow, naturally loose-tongued but made even more so by drinking, offered up a riotous jingle about a commoner who took liberties with one of the Queen's maids in waiting. And I would consider the likelihood that the thought of taking liberties with the Queen's maid really signified the thought of taking liberties with the Queen; while the thought of thus encroaching upon the Queen signified in turn the thought of dishonoring the King, but with one notable distinction: That whereas such an implicit reference to the Queen might indicate a purely lubricitous imagining, the thought of taking liberties with the King might rather signify a civic stirring. I cannot at this time be certain. But I am looking into this possibility with the patience and caution you have taught us to exemplify in our ministry to you.

The Messenger wrote more in this rich vein, until it came time for him to have his morning orange juice, and soon thereafter happily to undergo, with his usual regularity, his body's major unburdening for the day. So let us leave him to his gracious tasks and solemn enjoyments, while we turn aside, to raise our voices in exaltation and exulting:

Incipit vita nova, we exclaim. *The new begins all over. Begins all over where? Begins all over again.*

See how song touches all in pleasant painfulness, with its tasty odors. O lovely Garden of Pure Confusion. O Paradisaic Tower of Babelization. O Fall into Eden.

True, Good, and Useful Beauty — all hail to thy Circling Four-Fold Three-ness.

Flowerishes

Flowerishes

HE CAME TO HER THROUGH NEITHER RAIN NOR SNOW NOR HEAT NOR GLOOM OF NIGHT NOR THROUGH ANY OTHER BLOCKING THAT COULD STAY SWIFT COURIERS FROM THE COMPLETION OF THEIR APPOINTED ROUNDS.

He had learned how to be one of those simple, wholesome people who stay sane by driving other people crazy

To him, machinery was like a relative; you cussed it, and always gave it another chance

a friend is one who, if he wants a job done, offers you five bucks where he'd offer his enemy a hundred

he resolved always to wait two weeks before committing suicide

And when the clock strikes twelve, may it not strike you.

We moderns are not head-hunters; but we like to collect the heads that head-hunters hunted.

RATHER THINK ABOUT THE RULES OF RULE THAN BE A RULER

He says "devil" ten times, and "God" once, and calls it religion

he despised it as intensely as one school of perverts despises another

One must learn to be just morbid enough.

DIGNITY: STUFFING THE STUFFING IN A STUFFED SHIRT

in a world full of problems he sat doing puzzles

They got themselves good berths by policies that would sink the ship

It's bad magic to pick a fight, and sickening to avoid one

for one man to buck a bureaucracy is like punching a fog

"We're so excessively in love," he said: "You be my ultra-Violet, I'll be your infra-Red."

THEY LIKED TO SIT AROUND AND CHEW THE PHATIC COMMUNION

basic motivational problem: why does the chicken cross the road to get to the other side?

the man excused himself on the grounds that he must hurry home and change his long-playing record

Once women were so low in the social scale, as compared with men, that great savants debated whether woman has a soul. Now women have risen to equal status with men, and great savants debate whether anybody has a soul.

HE WAS NOT, LIKE THE MARXISTS, A TRAITOR TO HIS COUNTRY; HE WAS A GOOD SOUND PATRIOTIC CHURCH-GOING KIND OF CROOK

Pity the weeds in your garden, all trying to make an honest living.

when he didn't fight other people, he fought himself — and, boy! could he fight dirty!

as the man said when sealing a letter: spit on it and send it on its way

Flowerishes

Flowerishes

ven if you don't know him, you know he'd like to get more this year than he got last

frank, sincere, outspoken — clearly a security risk

as different as every moment of the day, and as unchanging as the centuries

dealing in guilt-edged securities

He learned touch-typing so that, while writing stories, he could look at himself in the mirror

retraced its course from sewer to source

on giving form to his life, he gave to himself,

and everywhere she went she took it with her

like putty in your hand, but wouldn't stay put

a true mystic, uniting opposites, he could sneeze "Gesundheit"

a grand- father clock, run by gravity

in imagery, a genuine imagician

WHATEVER PART OF YOU YOU STOP TO THINK ABOUT, YOU'LL FIND IT ACHING

stalagmites and stalactites, writing to join stalagmatites

everything but a life of her own has to Monica, who must remind herself to remind her boss

God his goal and goad
killed himself being the life of the party

her progress from socialist to socialite
the making-it-difficult dept.

a subversive belief in the perfectibility of man

elegance in a small apartment: putting on a record of the best music, to hide bathroom noises

"Lady, to insult you, but I don't mean could I borrow a match?"

hoping for golden opinions from leaden reviewers, enfolded in the big bosom of the Church a reformed drunkard,

ARISTOTLE, WHO BELIEVED THAT WE THINK WITH OUR STOMACHS, DIED OF DYSPEPSIA

a dual personality, she gave birth to twins

they canonize their saints

yours for fierce bunnies and sissified bulls going slow but still on the fast track

HE FELLED THE FOE WITH ONE SWIFT STROKE OF HIS ANTIMACASSAR

... words of tongue and pen, the saddest are these: "I knew him when ..."

"Here's a great opportunity; We'll arm you, put you right up front, and let you lead with your chin."

her war paint on, her lips as blood-red as though she were about to have a hemorrhage, her fingernails look-ing gorgeously sore, her face caked with a corpse-like ena-mel, she was all ready to be ardently desired

His friends said he could see around corn ers, his enemies said he had crooked visi

Flowerishes

Flowerishes

ness becomes a ritual than when ritual becomes a business ★ ersons in authority

better when busi-

Beware the Ideas of March

THE NEXT TIME THEY WANT SOMETHING, THEY'LL REMEMBER YOU FOR THE FORMER TIME — THANK YOU

Freud's theory of the father-kill may not be true of all, but it does seem true of Freudians

if they were getting along so well, why did one harp on the theme of killing rats, and why did the other keep spitting?

afraid of losing his faith in skepticism

THEY SAY ALCOHOL REVEALS OUR TRUE SELVES—BUT WHICH OF OUR SELVES IS THAT?

they were so keen on standardization, their women had interchangeable parts

On the good ship Squalling Brat, in a time of Crying Need

he said: "When I recall the Russian rape of Belgium in the first world war, and the Russian sneak attack on Pearl Harbor in the second, and how the Russians dropped the atom bomb on Hiroshima, I can certainly understand why our leaders should want us to arm Germany and Japan."

He ceased to follow the news, having found that, though he could not do much to it, it could do an awful lot to him

consider the plight of the harried exploiters who, in order to exploit a man, must sell him an electric refrigerator, a deep freeze, a washing machine, a television set, a new automobile before his old one wears out, a trip to Florida, a ton of magazines, etc., etc.,—and that's not all

The hard lot of the pro-ver-b-ial-ist

he could not read of an unsolved crime without feeling a strong desire to "confess" that he was the criminal; perhaps because the criminal was "wanted," and he wanted to be wanted

as they lay half asleep in the room, the sound of jays in the garden was like the scraping of carrots in the kitchen

Not knowing either how to live with money, or how to live without it

AS OUTMODED AS LAST YEAR'S MODEL OF THE UNIVERSE—I DREARY PLACE FUL OF OLD NEWTHINGS

the enemy was accused of "stirring up fraternization"

say "he is wrong," and they'll call you clear; say precisely how he is wrong, and they'll call you obscure

worry, my shorn darlings. For every one of you thus a-shiver on a bare hill in the winter wind, there is a wool-clad over-stuffed fathead even now miserably swel-tering in some over-heated city apartment."

the shepherd to his flock: "Don't you

when reading so religious-and-witty a poet as Herbert, he felt so virtuous-and-distinguished, he began consigning all sorts of people to hell

WAS AFRAID TO TREAT THEM WITH RESPECT, LEST THEY CEASE TO RESPECT HIM

on waited and are

They also serve, who only sit

★ the few teeth he had left, he ground them in his sleep ★ the toppling headstones,

Flowerishes

Flowerishes

ALONE, WITH STARS AND HORIZON, BY A HERMIT ROCK, OR WIDE WATER, OR A BIG BARE TREE — & ALL SET TO THINK PUBLIC THOUGHTS

EACH YEAR, MORE ACQUAINTANCES FEWER FRIENDS

AFTER FIFTY,
ONE FURTHER
THING TO
LEARN:
HOW RIPEN
WITHOUT
ROTTING?

good books, read rightly, will help you hold up your head, and not too high

you say "criticism of criticism," and they hear "fleas on fleas"

inherited several million dollars, plus Original Sin

THINGS AREN'T SO BAD. BUCK UP! PUT ON YOUR TEETH, AND GO OUT FOR A WALK.

PUT IN YOUR PANTS.

"I know my way around. I know what next!" he said. And echo answered, "What Next!"

THOUGH HE DESPISED ALL MANKIND, HE DEARLY LOVED AN AUDIENCE

the trouble with raising unanswerable objections is that people won't answer you

Three stages of universal history:
(1) "Be generous, let me in."
(2) They let him in.
(3) "Be picky, keep the others out."

all sitting prettily, in an ugly sort of way

it's hard to remember : but often all we need do is nothing

he held that poets were made for critics, just as sick people are made for doctors.

they used to say,

"Be as straight as a die." "Now, in the Hemming Way, Be as straight" "'Twas a bill."

it's not the snowfalls, however heavy — it's the drifts

tragedy helps us pity those we might otherwise envy or fear.

learn not to take umbrage, just penumbrage

An ecstatic snowstorm -- a grand dumping of pure white filth that made the whole countryside clean

He began by hoping to be heard, and ended by fearing to be overheard.

he felt it was alright to do like the others, if only he did it with a bad conscience.

resolved to love him, every time you found out all over again he was just something to take notes on

"Small craft warnings"—that's for YOU
Draw out the time. --and one part of an eddy going down stream might seem all your life to be going up stream

If a critic attacks you stupidly, give him a chance to forget it.

wearing her hat trimmed with mistletoe and spikes

Where many people might say, "It's six of one and half a dozen of the other," he would say, "It's either three biscuits or two triscuits."

The only civilized tempests are tempests in a teapot, like Shakespeare's

IS MORE IDEAS; AND THE CURE FOR ALL IDEAS IS DIGGING IN THE DIRT.

SEEING HOW HE TURNED HIS ENVY OF OTHERS INTO PRAISE OF THE LORD, YOU UNDERSTOOD WHY HE THOUGHT THE LORD WAS SO EAGER TO BE PRAISED BY THE LIKES OF HIM.

Flowerishes

Flowerishes

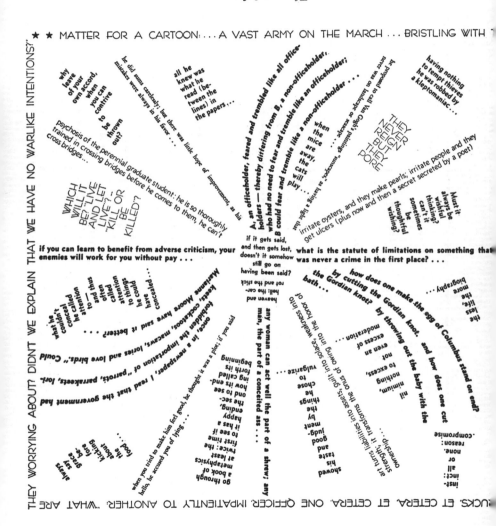

★ ★ MATTER FOR A CARTOON:... A VAST ARMY ON THE MARCH ... BRISTLING WITH

THAT WE HAVE NO WARLIKE INTENTIONS?"

THEY WORRYING ABOUT? DIDN'T WE EXPLAIN

why leave of your own accord, when you can contrive to be thrown out?

he did some carelessly; but there was little hope of improvement, as his mistakes were always in his favor ...

all he knew was what he read (between the lines) in the papers ...

B, an officeholder, feared and trembled like all office-holders — thereby differing from B, a non-officeholder; who had no need to fear and tremble like a non-officeholder ...

better was to propose to call Gogh's paintings works of torture; when the mice are away, the cats will play ...

having nothing to tempt thieves he was robbed by a kleptomaniac ...

psychosis of the perennial graduate student: he is so thoroughly trained in crossing bridges before he comes to them, he can't cross bridges ...

THEY NEVER PRODUCE THEREFORE POETRY

irritate oysters, and they make pearls; irritate people and they get ulcers (plus now and then a secret secreted by a poet)

WHICH WILL IT BE? "LIVE AND LET LIVE"? ... "KILL OR BE KILLED"?

Must it always be wishful thinking? can't it sometimes be thoughtful wishing?

if it gets said, and then gets lost, doesn't it somehow still go on having been said?

if you can learn to benefit from adverse criticism, your enemies will work for you without pay ...

what is the statute of limitations on something that was never a crime in the first place? ...

what he couldn't conceal he called attention to — and thus often called attention to things he could have concealed ...

Maitland Moore forbidden the cockatoos, macaws, lories and love birds." Could Keats' cockatoos have said it better?

Once, in a newspaper, I read that the government had forth its beginning ... how its ending called ... Now the sec-ond to see if it has a happy ...

rot and the stick hell: the car- and heaven

how does one make the egg of Columbus stand on end? the Gordian knot: by throwing out the baby with the bath ... by cutting the Gordian knot, and how does one cut

any woman can act well the part of a shrew; any man, the part of a conceited ass ...

go through a book of metaphysics twice: the first time at least to see ...

always kicked about the food for love

when you tried to make him feel good, he thought it not a peril; if not a plot, he thought it was

showed his taste and good judg-ment by the things he chose to vulgarize

moderation in excess, excess in moderation not even an minimum, nothing to excess,

ownership: as it turns liabilities into assets, guilt into solace of disparagement ... weakness into the honor into

inst-inct: all or none. reason: compromise:

the less the more biography ...

"WHAT ARE LUCKS, ET CETERA. ET CETERA. ONE OFFICER IMPATIENTLY TO ANOTHER, "WHAT ARE

SECOND EXERCISE FOR YEAR'S END

DECEMBER 31, MCM54

... something that you're going to be amazed how true it is ... something like clear sunlight maybe, slanting on crystal twigs, of a frosty morning, and after a dream of being snubbed by waiters. It was planned for midnight of a yearsend. Year-send? what sort of mission is that?

> Fall: I put 'em up. Who'll take 'em down?
> Spring: I take 'em down. Who'll put 'em up?
> O Bitter Recurrent Riddle of Storm-Windows.

You are a-guilt with hopes of preferment? You are a-grovel with undone self-love? That sinfulness you feel? Nonsense! It's but a body-odor or bad breath your friends won't tell you about—and they'll stop avoiding you, if you but buy the right bottle. Buy-o buy-o baby, on the installment plan.

The more he saw how things were shaping, the more he 'gan fershtay how the split between bourgeois and Bohemian arose in the first place. Byron, all is forgiven; but how did you get that passport? Back, back, back to La Bohême (with a difference)! Running around in circles, in flight from the wheels of technology. Confessing confusion at fission and fusion. (O fatal acrostic: nuclear, unclear. And in the custody of killers?)

Think how with all of whom I'm out of step with,
Think how of all the sleepless nights I've slep with!
How many bats are need to fill a steeple?
What makes me be such very awful people?
  Out of star-born into war-worn,
  Into the flat-tire of satire . . .

The questionnaire asked, in effect: "What sort of person are you?" Well, he happened to be the sort that's against answering questionnaires—but within the conditions of the contest, how could he say so? Let's start a Guild of the Bureaucratically Guilty, its members pledged always to answer these things wrongly, but never to admit membership. That's at least one thing could be cleared up.

All hail to the Three Great Modern Isms:
  Bureaucratism, and its counterpart, Cultural Toadying.
  Bohemianism, the only *remedy* for Bureaucratism. (We say *remedy*, since there is no known *cure*.) Hard-pressed, crowded into one odd corner of the mind—Walt Whitman with a crying jag.
  And third, running back and forth between Bureaucratism and Bohemianism, and arising in response to the general turn from Quest to Inquest: Informism.

O—right up out of from inside way down in under, I had those take-me-way-down-back-down-somewhere-or-other blues. Everywhere was loaded with things that would delight an imbecile, things to put around a Christmas tree for babies. And might we should establish a govt. bureau to keep stars from shooting out of season—then, with less unsafety, we could hang out our supermannish satellite, the mooniest moon.

> My country,
> Why be greatly famed for kill-stuff?
> My country, harshly by the news begoaded,
> Yankee (awake, and to thyself), come home.

Envoi:

I met a man who said: "We were climbing a steep hill. But just as we neared the ridge along the top, we paused to rest. While resting, we might have let our vision sweep across the broad valley that lay below us. But instead, though keeping the valley's presence so strongly in the mind's eye that we could almost literally see it, we gazed towards the ridge above and beyond us. And even as we watched, of a sudden there rose from the other side (which we had never seen!) the magnificently upright heads of a buck and his several does. We should have a word for that experience, in exactly that order."

He talked of a broad, horizonless lake, its water absolutely still, but with a gently sloping surface. "Limpid moveless water," he explained, "tilted slightly sideways. And when it freezes, O the ecstasy of skating from the upper end."

He explained how, without the slightest need for propulsion by one's own efforts, by merely holding the body in a fixed but comfortable position, one could go faster and faster and ever faster—for the lake extends forever, somehow circling back upon itself at every moment, whereby the skater need not strive again for starts. "O come skate with me," he said, "on the gently sloping lake."

He said, "We stand at the doorth of the year" (as though "door" were a verb, and he made a noun from the verb form, "dooreth," as with "warmth" from "warmeth," and "width" from "wideth," and "coolth" from "cooleth"). Thus, in his way, when thinking of year's end (the entrance to two-faced January) he spoke of "the doorth of the year." "Come, O come with me," he pled, "at the doorth of the year, to skate forever on the gently sloping, firmly frozen lake." And somehow placed a precious burden on my heart.

But, "No!" I de-reflectively answerved. "I'd like to let me linger yet awhile, whatever it may be my personal mooneth." Even now, at midnight, I await the beckoning morneth, when the sun comes uppeth, when the pink sun edges flatly above the skyline, comes up as bright and clean as a brand new dollar, as rash as a blast of unexpected music . . .

INTRODUCTION TO WHAT
Poems 1955–1967

INTRODUCTION TO WHAT

I

Wandering by a canal
Through meadows in a dream
Then later
Uninvited to a party,
Asking
"Where is the secret passage?"
   (which, when found,
   proved to be dirty and unusable—
   my coat dragging through the damnedest places)

I must read more Schopenhauer
   (him saying in sum:
"Will must blindly seek completion,
Life is sex, and Death excretion")

Remember how once snow-flakes
Stood still in mid-air,
The earth coming up to meet them?

Yet I've been different
Ever since I found
That snow is crazy.

II

A guy, let's say,
Starts out with curses
   (Not bloody—
Domesticated)

The threats of a mild fellow
He'd do no worse
Than knife you in the back
In social warfare
Hoping you'd find out
   (if he did a good enough job of it)
—if he really did knock you down
He'd be the first to pick you up

There's a beginning for you
That's how it goes.

> *All I ask*
> *Before I die*
> *All I ask is:*
> *Get that guy.*

'Nthen we could be pals.

The world gets gradually sprayed
With a hate-filled gospel of love;
And the number of the Beast is
Sex-Sexty-Sex;
And the fullness of the time of vengeance
Draws near.
Drink up, mine enemy.
Quaff a beaker of burning wrath,
While the whores of the press
Publicly boast of their Constitutional right
To be bought.

It's a wrangle
It's a tangle
It's a jingle jungle
    JANGLE
This world of Mr. Seat-Up and Miss Seat-Down
And their Ultimate Interminglings
While everything flows
    (*panta rhei* to you)

But how face death bravely
Unless it's exactly my kind?

III-a

loving poems, dreams, and similar psychanda

Living always on tenderhooks

thanking God who,
in his mysterious mercy,
taught the manufacture of pills
that man might have the gift of sleep

knowing that ailments
cost more than a trip to Europe

Respectful of primates
both simian and ecclesiastical

not yet psyched
    (his ego not yet massaged by an expert)

to avoid malice
praying that all his rivals
be received forthwith into Heaven

quick as a flask
pointpinning the genuwine patriot as
"One who swells with pride
Each time a chunk of the public domain
gets handed to a private corporation."

aware of the rat-race
in all walks of life
stumped by the pattern:
"They started it
By making us do it first."

grieved that his native tongue
has no rhymes for "rhythm" or "music"
and rhymes "song" with "wrong"

asking "Why praise a man
For sticking to his principles,
If they are sticky?"

Dear Reader
I make no claims
Except to say:
Where go next?

Abounding and abiding in
Foreboding—I'm gettn tired,
It's as simple as that.

Finding no difference
between suspicion
and love of knowledge

A D.F.S.
(Doctor of Fee-Splitting)

lostly forlorn
dejectedly cast down
contritely worn
innately to gloom inborn

Yet holding that
What gets said
With one less sound,
Is by so much
Toward beauty.

III-b

Inclined to bathe in bathos

Dreaming of betrothal in a brothel
While actually fighting
The battle of the bottle

Avowing acrostically:
"Let him who reigns
Resign."

Knowing that nothing
Is worth talking about
Except everything.

Looking upon all mankind
As brothers and sisters,
That is, in terms of
Fratricide and such.

Interested especially in the better of the new sciences:
Demonology, alchemy, toxicology, criminology, and of course
The new haruspicy, archaeology,
That prophesies old motives and ways of life
By systematic inspection of the entrails,
Studying ancient cultures' shit.

Slightly despising himself for sharing all the aims
That the pitchmen of this trick set-up
Tout as the glories of the profit system.

And above all
Concerned with these particular summations:
Yes, No, Maybe, Look, Huh?—and Please!

IV

On the theory of Rolling With the Punch,
Go view each mood
As aiming at similitude.
Thus, during a time of Wake-Wake, these beset me
　　("Several could stand to be upgraded," A Wall Street
　　　　friend will write):

as worried as a bug crawling across the floor
as fluttery as gas flames climbing on asbestos
as hopeful as packing
as true as a swat to the jaw
    (as clear as a cuss-word)
as aware as a man who finds he's been framed
as trusting as a sleepwalker
as uneasy as at the top (or anywhere else, for that matter)
as good-natured as an imbecile
as honest as a bandage
as frightened as a beard
as mum as a can of something
as charming as a young female skeleton covered with
        live flesh
as reliable as a bump on a log
as rotten as a well-digested dinner
as fertile as a weed-patch
as fertile as a pesthouse
as fertile as a neurosis
as run-down as progress
as crooked as you-know
as friendly as all get out

To which I later added:
as solemn as a rump
as non-committal as a ticket office (or a bed?)
as promiscuous as money
as sociable as a brush-off
as democratic as a sewer
as freedom loving as an intercontinental ballistic missile
as educated as one of Pavlov's dogs

Meet 'em halfway in premeditaysh,
By many guarding
Against each

V

Above all else remember:
Not just religion, but theology;
Not just theology, but theocracy.
To theocracy add the appropriate
Holy terrors and pious frauds—
Then you've caught up with politics,
Be its grounding godlessly here
Or Beyond the Behind the Beyond.

An enemy need but
Make mistakes in copying—
And history gets both born
And reborn.

Yes, No, Maybe, Look, Huh?—and Please!

> *let a little line of letters form your code*
> *let a little line of letters clear your road*
> *let a little line of letters*
> *help to free you of your fetters*
> *make you best among your betters*
> *and defray your debts to debtors*
> *let a little line of letters light your load*

Ah, unless love spurts like a gargoyle in a storm
It grows stony

Like with gazing on a Gorgon
　　(this the first law of generation and corruption)
Growing older, I think less vaguely of forgotten years
When down the long shafts of springtime
There blew a soft and playful . . .

If we grow too old to love truth
Might we still at least hate error?
And what is it when, sick deep inside,
The oldster grumbled,
"My guts have gone to pot"?

Yes, No, Maybe, Look, Huh? and Please!
To which by all means add
The deft poetess's
NEVERTHELESS

Forth to go with girded loins,
Upon your 'scutcheon, "Neanmoins."

VI

There are resources of this nature
To work around with:

Recovery from an illness
Relief by excretion or the kill
Release from a burden
　　(Getting out from in under)
Rain after drought (how eagerly it gets blotted up!)
Warmth after cold or coolness when hot

Finding one's way when lost
Bathing (in water) (in air)
Escape from a mean trap
From doubt   dejection   privation
To   certainty   joy   enough
Being fed when you need fed
In sum, from pain to pleasure

(Turns for Beatitudes
And *soon!*
With the enemy to rot henceforth in eternal torment)

happiness, noble birth, many and good friends, wealth, many and good children, mellow old age, health, beauty, strength, stature, athletic prowess, good reputation, good fortune, virtue, freedom, education, justice, courage, benevolence, philanthropy (says Aristotle, on the springs of the desirable)

aluminum ware, auto accessories, band instruments, bathroom accessories, china ware, cleaning supplies, clothing, cosmetics, deodorants, farm equipment, fertilizers, furniture, guns, heating equipment, household appliances, lawn equipment, lighting fixtures, office equipment, optical goods, paints, paper, photographic supplies, plumbing supplies, sporting goods, television, tires, toys, vacuum cleaners, ventilating equipment, washing machines, yard goods, youth furniture, zippers, zithers (says the mail order catalogue)

and a twenty-billion-dollar trip to the moon (says Kennedy)

Yours for The Light, the Doctrine, the Rebirth, the Promise, the Great Praiseworthy, the Over-Flowing Through Sheer Abundance, The Beginning-and-End-in-One, The Unfolding, The Homecoming, The Perfect Turn From Estrangement, the Revelation, the Moment Within the Moment (drawn out forever), the Ultimate, the Crossing, the Looking Back Into the Future and Forward Into Pastness, the Single Irreplaceable Meeting (the one-time miraculous combination, the very best of good luck), the Dirt Made Pure, the Flash of Blinding Super-Night, the Succession Jammed Together, the Forum of Sheer Form:

The Welling-Forth of Absolute Springtime, the Flowering in Winter, the Motionless Revolving, the Doctrine Without Dogma, the Law Without Lawyers, the Word Sans Syllables, the Grant Without Strings Attached, the King's Cameleopard or Royal Nonesuch (Ladies and children not admitted)

The sunrise at sundown, the New Forever Now

VII

You awful person,
How much you taught me,
You slovenly, poverty-stricken bastard,
You dirty guide,
You pilferer,
Crowding us into corners,
Cornering us in crowds

Hark, while I plunder harshnesses from the Pauline Apostle. Bah! There are those greedy of filthy lucre, blind of heart, alienated from truth, heady, highminded, lascivious, slothful in business, of cunning craftiness, given up to uncleanness, the double-tongued, those of darkened understanding, covenant breakers, without natural affection, implacable, unmerciful, deceitful workers, ministers of sin, transgressors, false apostles, adulterers, those given to idolatry, witchcraft, hatred, variance, emulations, wrath, strife, seditions, heresies, those who do not cast down imaginations, those who do not give cheerfully, those filled with all unrighteousness, fornication, wickedness, covetousness, maliciousness, full of envy, murder, debate, deceit, malignity, whisperers, backsliders, backbiters, the despiteful, the proud, boasters, inventors of evil things, adulterers, blasphemers, menstealers, liars, perjured persons, slanderers, brawlers, purloiners, thieves, traitors, those with the mouth full of cursing and bitterness, railers, drunkards, those of feet swift to shed blood (destruction and misery are in their ways), trucebreakers, false accusers, incontinent, fierce, despisers of those that are good, apostates, subverters, heretics (such as are condemned of themselves), lovers of their own selves, disobedient to parents, unthankful, unholy, extortioners, persecutors, partakers of other men's sins, those who wrong and defraud their brethren, those marked by filthiness, foolish talk, and jesting (rather than giving thanks).

In this realm of strife and vainglory, of much filthy communication among rulers of the darkness of this world, with its spiritual wickedness in high places, where novices are lifted up with pride, and men of corrupt minds, reprobates (teachers of the law, who do not understand what they say), exhort servants to be disobedient to their own masters and to answer back, many are puffed up, and have swerved aside into vain jangling, not avoiding foolish questions, and contentions, and vain, unprofitable strivings about the law, giving heed rather to fables and endless genealogies, proud, knowing nothing but doting about questions and strifes of words (perverse disputings of men of corrupt minds from which come envy, strife, railings, and evil surmisings), ever learning, and never able to come to the knowledge of the truth.

There are the effeminate, abusers of themselves with mankind, men leaving the natural use of women, and burning in their lust toward other men. And there are others which creep into houses, and lead away captive silly women laden with sins, led away with divers lusts.

And of women, there are wives who are not grave, not faithful in all things; they are idlers, tattlers, busybodies, wandering about from house to house speaking things which they ought not; and there are young widows that wax wanton, and women who do not learn in silence with all subjection, or who would teach, or usurp authority over a man, and are not silent.

In sum, there are the foolish, disobedient, deceived, serving diverse lusts and pleasures, living in malice and envy, hateful and hating one another for their envyings, murders, drunkenness, revellings, chambering, and such like, after hardness and impenitent heart, treasuring up unto the self wrath against the day of wrath, and thus, condemning themselves in judging others.

NEVERTHELESS

Yours for timorous stentorianism
Under the sign of
Yes, No, Maybe, Look, Huh? and Please

> *damya   diadamn   damlotta*
> *shanty   shanty   shanty*
> *let joy be unconfined.*

The rest is rest in silence
While on the underside of nowhere
Jes like nothn at all
It stands y-writ:

(Cætera desunt)

INTERLUDE

"Who are you?"
The sweet girl asked,
Her face twistedly bepuzzed.

I should say the truth, I don't know?
Or, in terms of insecurity,
"008 — 22 — 8559"?
Or my phone number:
Two billion,
Thirteen million,
Four hundred and seventy-three thousand,
Two hundred and forty-nine?

I gave the literal name—
And, passing, she repeated it.

Then, bethinking me, I turned and shouted after,
"But who are *you?*"
She called back,
"I'm Heidi."

Heidi, Heidi, Heidi,
Name-magic from out my childhood,
Mine Schweitzer Alpine Heidi,
And all this time a-hiding.

Name from the first of books
I ever loving heard,
In whatever of impermanence and changelessness
I have prayed, "God, drop me quick down dead,
If only others are not thus in jeopardy,"
The little girl called back,
"I'm Heidi."

COPYBOOK EXERCISE

I am looking for a book and not finding it
Now you don't have already the animals
Can you guess who is it?

See here the lady
The man is flying her kite
The man is stroking her kitten
He turns on her light
He fingers her mitten
The while she is knitten

I am looking for a book and not finding it
Now you don't have already the animals
Can you guess who is it?

The man rushes in, shaking hands hello
He is a paradoxer
Shouts hale and hearty
"Farewell! Good-bye! A Dios!
Auf Wiedersehen,
Arrivederci, au revoir,
And auld lang syne until we meet again,"
All the while shaking hands hale-fellow-well-met hello—
"Until we meet again."

I am looking for a book and not finding it
Now you don't have already the animals
Can you guess who is it?

114

(Come in out of the light
It might be bad luck
Come in out of the dark
It might be bad luck
Don't stay, don't go
It might be bad luck)

He phoned. Line busy
Phoned again. Line busy
Phoned once more. No answer

I am looking for,
and not finding,
the book

THE SPEEDING RAILROAD TRACK

(many of the ties need replacing,
and weeds grow among the cinders)

One day there was a railroad track
Went hurrying past a house.
It quickly sped away and back
As quiet as a mouse.

Where did it start? Where did it end?
I did not know.
But all at once around a bend
It would both come and go

And it would charge
Along a gorge
Like racing in a groove—
Yet did not move.

Three times a day there came a train
As noisy as a hurricane
And with its shrilling whistle
It made the whole world bristle.

And when some ducks nearby awoke
With quacks to match the quake
You could not hear a word they spoke
The whole place did so shake
And pound with one big sound.

The stir thus carried on
Until the train was gone.

Then everything would sleep again
And all a-glitter in the sun
The quiet track without its train
Was happy back and forth to run.

END OF AN ERA

So, now we've got another skunk.

Our old skunk died,
Of age presumably—
Near the end he'd come tottering towards you
Blindly in broad daylight.

Then we found him finished
By the wild azalea bushes—
Presumably a prize for something,
For soon after
He was gone for good.

Last night a new one
Proclaimed a New Order
With the Old Odor.

Old Skunky-Wunky and the Raccoon
Had been glum pals.
The raccoon would go right on eating
While the air was showered with unaimed threats,
A cursing without striking.

Of the pilferings,
Which blame for what?
"Damn those animals—
They think we're kinder than we are."

We have many little mutt-birds, too,
Among our retainers.
Sparrows and wrens dispute the back porch
And scold if you pause in the doorway
When there are young in the nest.

Feeling honored
We pay the taxes
For our forever scheming tenants.

But did that mosquito
Think I was being kind to her
Before I found her on my arm,
Sunk nearly to her eyes with feasting,

And I popped the deep-red capsule?

THE POET, ON HIS GRAND CLIMACTERIC

As love subsides, and I grow glum towards death,
And all the world to me seems progress-sick,
Each thing I do is proved impolitic,
Each thing I say I'd better saved my breath,
In this stark year my third and sixtieth.

Would that my pride like aching joints were swollen,
Then might I in my puzzlings be less sullen.

Almighty God, last night I damn near died.
A dream last night near threw me off the track.
Took me too near the other side.
O let me hurry back.

STAGES

(III)

He met her
At a perfect juncture of the year
When honeysuckle was flowering by the outhouse

(II)

But those other two:
They met on a fitful day of fever
That blew hot and cold.

(IV)

And me:
By a still pool,
Long after a waterfall—
The distance calling

(I/V)

whip-poor-Will
   whip-poor-Will
      whip-poor-Will

SAND, SEA, AND SKY

We comb the beach, as though to make us rich,
What with the gleaming southern sun to light us,
Driven among the shellshards by an itch,
A species of pruritis of detritus.

The spent wave (tumbling while the next one swells)
Dashes across the sand before retreating
Amid the hiss of water on the shells,
Or hiss of shells awash in water meeting.

We watch the burst of colors, soon to dim,
But still ablaze, trumpets in pantomime,
Here where, each day along the ocean's rim,
The sun goes down like for the last time.

VERSES FROM AMONG PROSE

(excerpted from "The Anaesthetic Revelation of
Herone Liddell," *The Kenyon Review,* Autumn, 1957)

I. From-What, Through-What, To-What

(1) Ducks quacking, dogs barking,
   A kitten scurrying for cover—
   And there he was.

(2) All day
   The songs, the games,
   The friendly altercations.
   "My compliments! My compliments!"

(3) A dim shape
   Borne away by shadows
   In the dead of night.

II. Prayer for Insomniacs

Great God, thy wondrous world is full of aches,
Of which a goodly share of them are mine,
On every side are proddings to mistakes
And most straight things get twisted serpentine.

Great God, the mass of miseries is deep,
And many are the wounds that will not heal.
But all I ask for me is: Let me sleep—
And Great my Lord my God, it is a deal.

III. Season Song

O when will the snow melt on the mountain:
The valley is now in heat.
And when will the heat of the valley go
The mountain snows to meet?

O once I went to the mountain
A feverish one to meet,
That we might go
As quick through the snow
As though to be in heat.

O I fear the time in the valley
When heat and cold have met
And the sun has set.

IV. Soma and Psyche

A Body's Platonic Converse With Its Soul

Soma, pleading:
    Inbeing,
    Flask without fault,
    Give   give,
    Until we melt.

    Now, beyond all thinking,
    Give towards an ultimate drinking.
    Give me unearned
    Thy chaliced selfhood towards me turned.

Psyche stirs ... Pause ... Then Soma resumes,
   more excitedly:
   What flower is this
   Unfolds in darkness as furtherance
   Of my mute ministering utterance:
   O—I would mount to depths,
   To drain full cups
   At near-collapse,
   To kiss
   A silken secret's lips.

Psyche, to herself, musing:
   Move,
   Be led,
   Let wings be spread
   To give,
   That he may love
   And dying live.

V. "One, Two..."

By the time he was two,
He had learned to buckle his shoe.

At the age of four,
He found something oddly revealing
   in the response he got
When he had knocked at a strange door.

Between the ages of five and six
He became a useful participant
　　　in the mysteries of fire-making
And often went forth to pick up sticks.

And by seven or eight
He was actually building usable things with them,
Laying them straight.

VI. Entrance, with Fanfare

Hornswoggle thus, you and all others of like ilk—
Hear now the words of Silkentine, and be
Content with golden laudability.
Whom should we stand at, whom against, and whom?
Braving their selves throughout all Christen-doom,
Gulp down hard liquor with their mother's milk.
Start stopping—spot like any run-down rebel
The eighty-seven ways of sitting at a table.
　　　(Bah! if the sea is restless, why in God's fair name
　　　Should *they* feel justified to petition
　　　　　for sound slumber?
　　　Consider me elsewhere . . .)
　　　　　　　　　　　　　exit, trampling

VII. Lame Quatrain

They're scattered 'cross the countryside
A long ways from the house.
So gather round the gadgets, girls,
And we'll all have tea.

VIII. Sea-Storm at Night

> Sound of sea-dream yonder
> The sea is roaring its own sea-monster
> It would pound its own waves down under

IX. Post-postscript

> To reach this front of sand-topped ridge
> We drove over a sunny clop-clop bridge

TRUE AND FALSE

At 63
You know by the feel
When the young dentist doesn't grip right.

Inexperience can make the gouging a botchery,
The fit a disgrace—
And you must foot the bill yet.

Your jaw the orphan's cheek
The barber learns on.

More epically,
Your jaw a trampled battlefield.

Begad, it's a god!
Those transcendently anaesthetized bones
Are a natural place alive—
Like mountains, volcanoes, caves personified.

We're a rich country
With much to throw away.
Me, for instance—
And old teeth.

(In my day I turned up what I could.
On the Seashore
I gathered shark's teeth,
Envying those oldest of old-timers
Who each year
Spit out crocks still firm
To grow a new denture.)

AFFLATUS

If there could be a big balloon
Of a sudden inflated
Noising for a time without loss of size,
Then collapses like a shot

Lies crumpled,
An old shoe-rag
In the corner of a closet—

That's the change
From doing a poem
To not ...

TRANSFORMATION

What made him rage so—
Powerful man with powerful horses
Plowing our garden—
What displeased him?

The memory escapes me
But I do know
That at his roar
I cringed beneath my smile
And paid him with alacrity.

No wonder I nearly passed him without recognition
When next we met
Some months after his accident.

Tossed roaring drunk over the handles of his plow,
Ripped by the steel like sod where he lay squirming
While his loyal team
Strained forward ...

Now but a fraction of himself,
Bent, shrivelled, and whining during the telling.

"It's lucky you had so much strength to spare,"
  I confided with a smile;
"A weaker man couldn't have stood it,"

  And held back my fist
  That might
  Crumple him like paper.

WHAT DO?

(What would we have us do—
We, like the traffic,
Our many little aims
Adding up to one big aimlessness?

Back to religion,
With holy terrors and pious frauds on one side,
And on the other, business as usual?

What pill can give us
A good filing system?
Ah, to be in hvn
Playing the crwth.)

SIX GRAMMATICAL CHARADES

Rule: Assume that, as in French, all nouns must
be either masculine or feminine, never neuter.

I

Bearing his riders with zest
He dashed through her fence
Across her flowers and bushes

Throbbing, veering, finally slowing to a halt,
While she could but lie there
And get torn.

No one, fortunately, was hurt.
They dragged him back to the highway—
And the gardner patched her up.

A few days later
When he drove past her again
You'd hardly know it had happened.

    (Car and Garden: The Accident)

II

His gales lashed her
He dug into her side
With wave tumbling atop wave—
Swirls seethed around rocks.

Later
The storm subsiding
She warmed to his sunlight—
The sea like a lake.

    (Sky and Beach)

III

She gave access
He was but her instrument.
Turn him
To open her.

    (Handle and Door)

IV

When he struck her,
In the heat of his attack
She clamored
And sparks flew.

    (Hammer and Anvil)

V

His mark upon her,
Though she said nothing
The situation spoke volumes

    (Print on a Page)

VI

Caught in her gutter
He pitched down her drainpipe
And bubbled in a barrel

    (Rain on the Roof)

AH! TO BE...

Ah! to be a movie queen's bodyguard.
To keep her books.
To sign her checks.
To threaten to blacken her eye.

> While living in lubricity
> We'd buy the best publicity.

Together we could get religion,
Could "breathe the air of other planets."

SOME METAMORPHOSES OF VENUS

A Medea in Old Greek
Made virgin again in Church Latin
Corrupted in Baudelaire's French
In Spanish immured
In Italian voluble
In metaphysic German, an *Urform*

In the vernacular
The glow and glue of gloveless love

MORE METAMORPHOSES OF VENUS

I — Oneiric Translation

He upstairs fell out of bed,
Bumping his head on the floor.

She downstairs, at the thump of his head,
Dreamed that he knocked on her door.

II — Wrapped Gifts

Insofar as all the boxes under a Christmas tree
Could be called sisters
"Open me first" would be written on
The oldest sister-box

III — Ailments

Some suffer from *tædium vitæ,*
Some from *angina pectoris,*
And I knew a young couple
Subject to severe intermittent attacks
Of *argutatio lecti.*

IV — Elderly Couple's Romance
Begins Over Card-Game

It was quite late, but nonetheless
He said "Wed?" and she said "Yes."

Both said, "It's good to be alive,"
He 96, she 85.

Their hands had touched and laid love bare
In a game of double solitaire.

INVITATION À CYTHÈRE

> free translation of Goethe's *Kennst du
> das Land,/Wo die Zitronen blühn?*

I know a magic spot
Let's both go there—
A speechless land of not,
With ferns like hair.

It is a flower
A lace-trimmed power
Illusion
And seclusion

The homely home of beauty—
Think what chores
Are done with love and duty
By its shores!

So let us linger both
About this place*
Huddling close
Beyond the lace.

---

* Mallarmé refers similarly to an *étrange bouche.* He describes it as *pâle et rose
comme un coquillage marin.*

APOSTROPHE: ON BEING HAPPY

Happy am I you quickly went your way
And left the room all empty where you sat.
Happy am I, I knew you but a day
Or rather, but an hour or two of that.

Happy am I, I did but touch your hand
And touched it as a mere formality.
Happy am I that all remarks were banned
Such as might be exchanged absorbingly.

Happy am I in this frustrate design
Which I must bear as my good-fortuned cross.
Happy am I that you were never mine,
To make me dread the terror of your loss.

THE PROTECTION OF PROPERTY

And what if things got
To where she might exclaim:
"Why! Mr. Bloop!"
And not from malice either.

(Q: "And do you know
What Mr. Bloop did?"
A: "No—
What did he dood?")

Well, the old deadhead fuddy-duddy
Daddy-doodled,
For she had warmed
The hardles of his gog.

Were she outside
He might have proffered:
"Could I show you
My severe monastic cell,
My religious etchings,
And what it's like
To lie on my bed of nails?"

But no—
There she was,
Already in his room,
Having brought him flowers
And a vase to put them in.

Some were near dead,
She noted in distress.
"Naturally," he put forward;
"They're day lilies—
And it's near sundown.

"But let me walk you to the corner.
I need the air."

To the corner, then—
And so,
Good-bye to another one.
Warm vibrancy,
Good-bye.

R. R. STATION

In the Waiting Room—and oof!
Across from where I sat,
Definitely a packaging job,
With bright colors designed to catch the eye
And a handy device for easy opening.
So bulging with *Frühlingserwachen*
She all but stepped out of her clothes.

Very leggy—
And towards what?

The *terminus ad quem* in that terminal
Was a gent of about her age,
And responding earnestly.

No new angle here.
But wait.
Next her was her luggage—
And next to that
Unmistakably
Sat Momma.

Even while there transpired
The would-be giving and getting,
The daughter traded words with Momma,
Who doubtless wasn't just seeing,
But remembering.

Until as preordained
There barked a muddled, mechanical proclaiming—
And the team
Went high-heeling off,
Jerkety click-click,
After one last
You-know-and-I-know
Interchanged anonymously
   (or do I mean universally?)
Btw. daughter and young gent.

A bit later
The speak-machine made similar but different
        overlapping sounds.
So, interpreting correctly,
Picking up books and papers
I trundled to the platform
And made   my train

ABJECT COMPLIMENT

For her
It was as simple as this:

To fib, to pilfer,
To idle, shirk, maliciously gossip,
And all the while be loved
For sheer loveliness.

MORALITY PLAY

Dragon flies,
in one hell of a tandem

The fun's over
but the intimacy perforce drags on
while she lobs him across the water.

If only someone had told him!
He's stuck with this kid right—
And he'd as lief
Be dragged by his tongue.

THE INITIATION

See how the dancers, looking like naked, handle one another
The big he-dancer has a zucchini in his tights

What do they all dance about?
The pretty girl-dancers all dance about the big he-dancer
And about how a novice is getting initiated
Into some mysteries.

She is to learn their same secret
Like when the big he-dancer carries her off behind the wings
And she comes back changed to look like all the other girls,
Her white now red.

All are *glad* that she should join
The band of votaries with the big he-dancer.

The pretty novice lies down with legs spread
It's part of the service
Just before the curtain falls

It was an idea worked out by the big he-dancer
Whose wife looks worried and has three kids

ONE FOR THE ROAD

He being new to the place
She knowing it well
Friends had her drive him there

But where was it!
She passed the turnoff going north
Passed it again on the way back

Distressed
By the lostness
She begged "Don't tell them"

He said sure, and went on making conversation.
She said she loved to "go go go"—and sometimes
"Just *give myself* to the road."

    (He'll be cautious, dear Soft-Shoulders
He'll watch out, nice Cattle-Crossing
Lovely Side-Road
Falling Rocks   Yield
Sweet Slippery-When-Wet)

TO THE MEMORY OF e. e. cummings

If there is an ultimate Enormous Room
may you find it equal to your skills as fantasist.

Cummings, bright boy until the very end.

You knew damned well
how to turn a private compliment
universally—
    (girl, moon, body, and the learned complimenter
masking as naive)

You put happily together
green, gold, silver, dawn,
horn, four lean hounds,
and of course a "swift sweet deer"

your "heart fell dead." It really did.
stopped by much more brain than you'd admit to,
you secretly, like the scholastics' God,
an intellectual.

You talked of fruit like dangling participles
  your heart knowing
"the bulge and nuzzle of the sea."

 gladly you professed yourself
"mud-luscious," a "balloonman"
"goat-footed"
 in spring.
 You knew how to give a poem the works.

True, you railed against "fingers of prurient philosophers"
that "pinched and poked"—
as out of line with your cult,
the rhythmic, lover's laying on of hands.

You knew the "great writhing words" of jealousy, too,
and the song that might stand for such
when you hear it back
out of an unseen bird.

you kept looking for life
and finding it
all except the last time

you liked the rain
that necessarily makes the flowers grow
and a fortiori you wrote in sweet lewdness of flowers
whether uncut or deflowered

"Spring is like a perhaps hand,"
You insisted.
Gad, that alone could kill a man!

nephesh psyche anima soul—
ruach pneuma spiritus spirit—
we can't always know for sure just which is which
but this is certain:

tu as rendu l'esprit
toi qui avais de l'esprit (humeur, caractère)
toi esprit-de-vin

toi esprit fort
      (du latin, spiritus, souffle,
substance incorporelle,
être imaginaire,
comme les revenants, les génies, les sylphes, les gnomes, etc.)
without spirit, you would say nothing
when sans spirit, then sans espoir,
then you'd slink away, begone
you and your lower-case highly individualistic i
like Emerson a much-seeing eye aye-saying

You liked the design
of a "born failure"
who solved it all
by starting "a worm farm."
and at the risk of the obvious
you refused not to say that a naked pretty girl
"is worth a million statues."

No solemn would-be Neo-Metaphysical
ever hammered more on one metaphor
than you obscenely likening the first night
to starting a car—
or you could reduce the process
to a jaunty dialogue

no comedy of manners ever outpointed you on the
"brand of marriageable nymph which is
armed with large legs rancid
voices Baedekers Mothers and kodaks."

sorry even into eternity for self-soiled drunks

eater of flowers

too patriotic not
to despise the pat rhetoric of patriotism
too accurate
in your vision of mankind befouling the nest.
hence vs. "punks of Progress."

speaking slyly
of a lady's
"Etcetera"

much at one with a mouse as Burns
but with fancier moralizings

piously grateful to a pillow that had been
                experienced intimately
thinking of your nephesh psyche anima soul
as a "ragged meadow,"
preferably in springtime

making not amends, but at least as much as a good poem can,
to big Olaf, the tortured "conscientious object-or"

sure at the time that each time is the best ever

saying things that could be answered only
by being there
in silence to be touched

condescendingly humbly twitting "little joe gould,"
letting him share your lower case

with epigrammatic jingles and entêtement
conceding to the "kumrads"
nothing but the cult of hate

saluting "a disappearing poet of always,"
whom other than yourself?

You did unfew unold things indeed with un

caught in being continually against sameness
and its nest of bowls of sanctions

responsible first of all to fillip and flick and click
and to the turn that in turn turns on itself
    (if need be, let the rest take care of itself)

but when you say
"above all things be glad and young,"
that's what to tell a poem,
damn it,
not a person

    (as death follows age and age follows young
so ding leads to dong and dong leads to dung)

finding in fragments of nonsense jingles
asteroids of the First and One Philosophy

often you'd rather lean on a window sill
than go trampling through a door

saying not a thing's "appearance" but its "seem"—
calling the mores "the was of shall"
yet reducing the poet's job to
XAIPE rather than "have fun"

believing first in
"one good yes"
along with your incessant
unnishness

made light like flowers
by the silent song of children
carved out of stone

lying as valiantly atrociously as a martyr,
about love   love   love

sometimes in effect saying
say it first and find out afterwards

a salesman selling anti-salesmanship

bopping politicians
yet making things much less tough for them
than they do for one another

as cunning as the devil
in saying that war is hell

quite aware
of Miss America's rape by Progress

holding that love comes by being let go
calling love yes,
and ably
from out your unnery

Putting forth a Shakespearean sonnet
about "true lovers,"
though tricked out with typical cummings and goings-on

working at all hours
with more starts than bees darting from a hive
   (non nova sed nove)
to show how springy spring is
risking new wordy ways for a neo-archaizing primer to say
it's good to be alive
and nature heals
and "we are in love" said twistedly

calling Jesus Christ what others have called the devil:
namely: lonely

of flowers and girls and artifice and children (at a distance)
and eternity (close up) and morning
and the menstrual new moon
and ad interim qualified delay of death
and artifice and flowers and girls and artifice

until the untilled land
beyond the last crossing over into
the non-undeadness of an
obituary

PRAYER OF THE NEWSPAPER EDITOR

I pray thee, God,
Send us for tomorrow's copy
Some great flood, or earthquake, or disastrously
        erupting volcano
Or picturesquely havoc-bearing storm
Or other natural calamity such as we
In piety
Call "acts of God."

Or at least, I pray thee,
May there transpire some big new step towards
        greater global malice
Or may the peaceful work of the U.N.
Be disrupted by a new flare-up, with corresponding walk-out.

Or may some general or admiral decide to blowhorn
About our ever-mounting power
To spread universal misery.

Or, if there is to be no true disaster for this day
Then I pray thee
Send us at least conditions making for some dreary rumor
That we may flaunt it before the nation
In foot-high, front-page headlines
    (Being to truth dedicated
We can deny it later
In a small item well-hidden)

Give us, I pray thee,
Some such monstrosity
As a way of drawing gapers to market
That our merchants may the better peddle their wares.

And then, happily,
Many thousands more acres of stately trees
    (Such as young Keats called "solemn senators")
Trees that make a Cathedral of the forest,
Will have been successfully processed,
Transformed into the yellow matter of journalism,

By the rules of hygiene
To use once and throw away.

A LETTER FROM THE CENTER

Some time back, our hero had the good fortune to spend a year in residence as a fellow at the Center for Advanced Study in the Behavioral Sciences, Stanford, California. By the rules of the game there, he was free to think, write, talk, listen, and of course argue, to his heart's content (and all "on the house"). While he was thus in the thick of this rich dream life, a fellow-Fellow, member of a "grievance committee," came to interview him, asking if he had any grievances he wanted presented to the administration. Whereupon our hero exclaimed, "Grievances? My God, I'm in Heaven!" Then he wrote these lines, the words in romans representing the mad world of everyday, the words in italics being as though sent back from the delightful Beyond.

> Ophelia (*alone*):
> See now, how goes it with the sidleclove
> In all its massive splendor.
> Dear love, sweet love, great problematic love,
> I would not, no nor anything
> How that the day be sweet.
>
> Come! Come! What time is this,
> With eyes of houses, and mother-bodies . . .
>
> Hush! Do not stir the king,
> Who reads on peace of mind and
> bourgeois etiquette.
>
> What was that distant tremor?
> An earthquake on an enemy satellite?

Or someone suddenly decides to buy?
Or you and that other business—
You didn't after all—
Imagine! you had been but dreaming!
Like a dried oyster, served warm with talk
At cocktail hour.

Oh, I am sick,
With Progress
And hellish more to come.
The letter! I had forgot the letter!
See what it says here:

In our elevation above the century—
Each Fellow's cell having one wall all glass
Giving upon some millions of square miles of
          geologic marvels—
We fly about
Playing on golden harps
Amid flower-beds
And winding walks
And conferences on the sad state of
          aberrant mankind
There below.

He is joking!

My friends there with you—
Tell them we are watching,
And our gaze is kindly, Yes.

Tell them to go in sureness.

Tell them it is writ:
All will turn out well. Yes.

DER TAG

Therc's a lotta meanness loose in the world
O when that lightning strikes
There's a lotta hatred squirmin around
O when that thing goes off.

There's a lotta flags unfurled in the world
O when that moment strikes
There's a lotta vermin squirmin around
O when that thing goes off.

O when that thing goes off
O when that thing goes off
Let me be gone the day before
Than when that thing goes off.

PATTERN FOR A POEM

The drive succeeded
The quota was filled
The deal was put over
He got the job

O let me break down and weep

The greatest nation since the death of Christianity
Piles a-plenty of bombs and the goods to deliver 'em
The richest churches
Rivers polluted with the filth of the world's
          mightiest industries
And from all quarters of the globe
The newest facts daily to keep men goaded.

While the dignitaries sit on their dignities
O let me break down and weep.

  (Pattern for a poem:
Boast of imperial greatness,
Then end on lamentation)

ZIGGURAT CITY

During his long exile from the court
Ovid suffered imperious, imperial sorrow.
Hence the *Tristia*.
And you, when you loved night lights
And dreamed
Of living edified in a penthouse

With your own lawn up there
And a garden gate
And maybe a cow

That's how you could have owned the city—
Stinking
Squirming
Noising
Babylonian
Ziggurat City.

CIVIL DEFENSE

No first-class war can now be fought
Till all that can be sold is bought.
So do get going helter-skelter
And sell each citizen a shelter
Wherein, while being bombed and strafed, he
Can reek and retch and rot in perfect safety.

DIDACTIC AVOWAL

Great God, grave fount of universal grace,
Great God, the source of perfect blessedness,
Great God, thy godam stupid human race
Is kicking up one devil of a mess.

Great God, I know this is no time to scoff,
But why not let us call the whole thing off?
Thy dismal creatures, in their I.Q. teens,
Can but tear things to holy smithereens.

Great God, on one occasion waking early,
I saw again a misty dawn and pearly—
And in my having had this chance to scan it
I saw close up the beauty of thy planet.

Great God, if all gets blown to smithereens,
It will be done by thy loved ones' machines.

THE GREAT DEBATE

A struck match
that flares up
and goes out,
a dud ...

Slow down the psychology of time—
and that flash that fizzles
lived to a ripe old age,
died in its dotage.

To expunge a one-day fly
be quick.
Spare it interminable seconds
of long-lingering torture.

Some would treat life like a political football
and let lawless nations
shoot their way into the U.N.
Others would sweep it under the rug.
But life is in reality
a spate of hard-core boomerangs
at the crossroads.

Life needs an agonizing reappraisal
if we are to protect our national posture
and its image

But time is running out.
Where we but increase our forces
the enemy escalates.

Give us an honorable peace
And we'll stop
Our dishonorable war.

(There's shouting in the streets—and I wanna go home)

TO CULTURE

"And now it is the time" ...

Said not as at the moment of vengeance
Nor of acclaim
Nor as one climber to his companion when the peak is
    reached
Nor as the king to his warriors
On the eve of battle

But as by one who,
Even as I,
Now here alone at last with you,
Beyond all things that might impede between us—

"And now it is the time."

Culture,
Loveliest
of all
Tax-dodges,

For thee
I will do my best,
What with my dying revolver.

In times of septuagenary drought
May things grow green
With brisk financial downpour.

RHYMES DONE WITH AID OF A COMPUTER

Tell me what to do, and I'll do it if I can,
I'm a truly independent modern man

Put me in traffic, I'll keep to the right
Give me a radio, I'll turn it down at night

Supply me with a questionnaire, and I'll fill out the form
Tell me what's abnormal and I'll try to be the norm

Show me a slot machine, I'll drop in a coin
Whatever club will have me, I'll pay my dues and join

If you tell me something's stupid, then I'll assume it's nerts
If I am asked to give and give, I'll give until it hurts

Jot me down some figures, I'll add up the sum
Give me nail and hammer, I'll doubtless hit my thumb

Show me the stairs, and I'll walk up and down
Show me the by-pass, then I'll avoid the town

Tell me not to hurry, I'll not arrive too soon
You beat out the rhythm, I'll hot-foot to your tune

Tell me where the line starts, and I'll go stand in line
Tell me what the fine is, and I will pay the fine

Tell me what to do and I'll do it if I can
I'm a truly independent modern man

EDITORIAL—ON A CRIME AGAINST DARWINISM

Billions
To back our ways
In lands for which they are unfit

To prop up misfit outfits
That can at best last as long
As U.S. foots the bill.

Given the nature of things
It's a hose down a rat-hole
It's to set to sea in a sieve

Till the bowels of Fort Knox
Rumble as hollow
As Mammoth Cave

CAESAR'S WIFE

"If that is my office,
If I was born to be above suspicion,
I will accept those rules."

That's what I said and did—
And kept my counsel.

But if
On one occasion
In the abandon of the Saturnalia
If in disguise
I gave myself to many among the filthy,
And in that one transgression
Felt cleansed for all a lifetime

Who should speak ill of me?
Have I not nonetheless contrived
To carry out my role,
Helping uphold the State with ceremony?

And I bore Caesar no bastard—
For his dear son was already in me.

OF ROME AND CARTHAGE

Summoque ululavit vertice Nymphae
Aeneid, IV, 168

It is explained in Virgil's book
How Dido gave what Aeneas took.

While they lay sheltered in a cave
Aeneas took what Dido gave.

At first things were doubly tactile,
Then eventually contractile.

Aeneas and Dido, in stormy weather,
Put their snails together.

A CITIZEN LOOKS AT THE FEMALE FIGURES
ON AN ANCIENT JAR

He'd have been gentle
Owning you,
Dead slave girls—
Always he'd have been
Like saying please.

You maybe even—
After a fashion—
He'd have let
Be tyrants.

Three days each month
He'd have done the singing.

Oil-scented
Flutterlike
Secretly germ-laden

Brought from what far villages?
How tested by experts?

Prime matter of motherhood
Forever unpossessed in life
As now in death—
Toys for a king-sick king.

VERNEINUNG DER VERNEINUNG:
ERGÄNZUNGS-BEDÜRFTIGKEIT UND
HOFFNUNGSPHILOSOPHIE

für Ernst Bloch

von Klaus Burg

Was Drüben giebt es hier und dort?
Wo ist der Menschheit Standesort?
Was, ausser fruchtbar furchtbarer Angst und Beschwerde,
Ist für uns Arme das Erbe der Erde?

Gelitten hat man alles was man leiden musste—
Ganzheit, Seele, und das Unbewusste?
Sag' doch: Wann kommt's, wann bricht's,
Das Licht des bisher unentdeckten Anti-Nichts?

Hoch Hoffnung! Im Exil der ewigen Vorgeschichte,
In Wachtraum und Wachtthurm schreib'
        deine Entlastungsgedichte.
Singe darein wie ein Urwunsch hold und zauberweich
Die Proklamierung von der Heimkehr in das
        letzte Messiasreich...

---

* Built around Bloch's terminology, as indicated in an article on him in *Deutsche Zeitschrift für Philosophie* (1958). I regretted particularly that I wasn't able to work in: *geistentleert, irre gemacht, Weihrauch, ungelungen, Inbegriff, Grundbetrieb, Bestimmung,* and *Sendung.*

LEBEN WEBEN SCHWEBEN STREBEN
GEBEN UND VERGEBENS DOCH AUFHEBEN

Die Ur-Uhr ist so immer irgend-weit
Sie ist das Nunc der Mythos-Ewigkeit
Ohne Bewegung zählend stets die Zeit,
Während *ex nihilo* der Geist sich giesst
Und Goethe-strebend in den Raum zerfliesst.

Woraus entsprungen endlich, wie misslungen?
Ein Kind des uralt daurnden Ur-Jungen,
Das Heute ist ein Grobian—
Und grosser Ekel greift mich an

ON PUTTING THINGS IN ORDER

File this, throw out that.
Alert the Secretariat
In re each claim and caveat
To better serve the Cause of Alphabet.
Throw out this, file that.

File this, throw that out,
We know beyond all doubt
how Perfect Order reconciles—

And now throw out the files.

A GO-ROUND NOT MERRY-

to headquarters (query)

just because you happened to suspect him
of suspecting you
of being a Secret Agent
why break off all connection just for that (query)

at the very least
he most likely gives you credit
for selling out to both sides
quite as
in his twistedness
he could sell out
to neither.

but if you will no longer
have truck with him
how else can he count
on getting his views
reported back (*da capo*)

OLD NURSERY JINGLE BROUGHT UP TO DATE*

If all the thermo-nuclear warheads
Were one thermo-nuclear warhead,
What a great thermo-nuclear warhead that would be.

If all the intercontinental ballistic missiles
Were one intercontinental ballistic missile,
What a great intercontinental ballistic missile that would be.

If all the military men
Were one military man
What a great military man he would be.

If all the land-masses
Were one land-mass
What a great land-mass that would be.

And if the great military man
Took the great thermo-nuclear warhead
And put it into the great intercontinental ballistic missile,
And dropped it on the great land-mass,

What great PROGRESS that would be.

---

* The original of this unwieldy transformation is as follows:

    If all the trees were one tree
    What a great tree that would be.

    If all the axes were one axe
    What a great axe that would be.

    If all the men were one man
    What a great man he would be.

    And if all the seas were one sea
    What a great sea that would be.

    And if the great man
    Took the great axe
    And chopped down the great tree
    And let it fall into the great sea

    What a Splish-Splash that would be!

DAWN IN AUTUMN IN VERMONT

About the new sewage-disposal plant,
I had asked what allowance was made
for increase of population; and the old-
timer answered: "Vermont is shrinking."

Dawn clear above bare trees—
Night lights of distant village linger
Belatedly towards day.

Cock crows much as of yore.

(That's where I'm now at,
at this early hour.
I'd rather be asleep yet,
But you can't have everything.)

O cleanly sparse Vermont
In leaf-down autumn.

Some places are so up and coming
It's like the end of the world.
But in Vermont
The falls splash by weedy factories
Run once by water
Then by steam
Then by electricity
And now, praise God, often not run at all

The towns dwindle,
And reborn nature
Grows rank in sloping cemeteries.
Industry dies
That once again
The streams may quicken
With the strike of decent trout.

Life graveyard-lovely
In Greenmount

   (Of memories
Of schools
Of sources returning)

"Vermont is shrinking"—
The God-damned industries
Thrive better elsewhere.

All shrewd wisemen
Should buy into Vermont.

EJACULATIONS ANENT A
      FLAMING CATASTROPHE
      (to view things simply yes, just as what is)

Strike up the band—let's all be doing the same
But what?

Flames lick up and down the adjoining canyons
with apocalyptic glows and spurts at night—
and a dust settles about us, as though spewed from a volcano

The sky is aglow
there is a rain of parched Vesuvius-ash all about us

You should see what can be done
To make the sky red with mountainsides

The dry slopes are tender with tinder
and at the slightest touch they yield
—flaring

Among the more recondite problems
count bordering areas invaded
by snakes and burned deer

If the blaze was set by an arsonist,
as one thing led to another
his whimper must have ended with a bang
Or what does happen to such odd creatures
when finding themselves thus expressed by proxy?

178

My sense of simple parsimony was outraged (stop)
Yet, granted, there was a grandeur
In the sweep of calamity all across the sky (stop)
To that extent was I, then,
Kindred with the kindler?!

Gnaw!
I fear it all started
Not with some morbid baystard in need of reassurance
slinkingly
Rather it got here
through sheer lack of imagination,
the inability to glimpse beforehand
what leads to what
under circumstances in which a match was dropped
by such a one of us who
except for what a moron can buy boxes of in a supermarket
couldn't strike up a fire
no matter how ardently he tried (stop)

Mankind's worst enemy
just good old normal human *Dummheit*
and always with us
(stop, if possible)

> [Thoughts on a costly fire that spread through
> the mountains like wildfire]

AT YOSEMITE

These Falls—
What all falls with them?

(Not that stunted pine
In the cleft of a cliff?)

They're like spilling
From a hole in the heavens

Spilled goblets,
Plunging from layer to layer

About the edges of your stare
The cliffsides levitate

(The water, falling, stops—
The moveless mountains rise)

Watch the water's lace get ripped
In spurts like rockets.

(That overhanging chunk, laden with centuries,
The gouge of the next ice age will bring that down.)

Borrowed greatness
Of feeling puny among heights

All prior to pollution
Except maybe for Strontium 90 in the snow-water

And it costs several thousand a year
To gather the tincans scattered along the paths

   (Each visitor must leave his *grumus merdae,*
His sign that King-Kill Kilroy was here)

As you come closer
The sight adds sound

Or is it the roar
Of your own blood in your ears?

Down here, in early twilight afternoon,
Up there, pinkly a-glow, the sun on snow

Looking up,
Let's drink to the falls

Our bodies incipiently leaping
Our bodies incipiently pissing

And what of all was mostly mine?
In the cleft of a cliff, a stunted pine.

   (Hang on, old boy!
Yes, I see it now.
Maybe I tried too hard.)

INNS

Once near a model motel
We found a stone phallus
   (Worn smooth by the friction of the sea).
I brought it home,
But didn't know what to do with it.

For the old Greeks,
Death the truly hospitable inn-keeper—
Since he welcomed all.

Maybe Chaucer's inns
Weren't as winsome
As you might imagine—
But I hope not.

The idea of a perfect inn
Might make you travel all life long
In search of one
Always out looking for inns
   (Until you find the Greeks').

Luxury hotels
May be a species of despair.

In the Rockies is a place
By a torrent cascading from away up
As though in haste
To bear a message.

L'AUBERGE

"Note, far below, the little chain of lakes
  Connected by a twisting river.
  And this inn seems so pleasant,
  Why not stop here for the night?
  Viewed from this turn
  The sunset should be an oratorio.
  This should be the place."

The grey man had spoken softly to his companion
Who nodded assent.

Still early afternoon—
But far below,
The chain of lakes
Lay twisting in velvet shadow.
Up here
The light was clear and crisp,
Yet gentle.

For arrangements
Few words were needed—
Then the two were in their room
In quietude.

Or was it quietude?

From somewhere about the inn
Came a steady voice
Tense

Yet so remote
It made the scene
(The scooped-out valley,
The tilting wall of mountains,
The road that curved up to this destination)
Doubly silent.

Their room faced west.
(He must not miss one moment of that sundown.)
And having poured tinkling drinks
They sat by the window
Watching a high hawk soar below them.

Now he could hear the voice more clearly
But from where? And about what?
Was it straining in argument?
Occasionally it stopped—others took over—
But they were conversational,
Less urgent.

The sound came from above? Below?
Once he walked about the corridors, probing,
But always, though near at hand,
It seemed from somewhere else.

"Surely it's the voice
Of a man much younger than I," he reasoned,
"And absurdly urgent.
But anyhow . . ."

Returning to his seat by the window,
Looking out aimlessly, he mused:

"In the inner slopes and vistas of the years,
How still the vague but deep-down memory
Of one's own earlier selves?"

HERE AND NOW

(An old man, to himself):

While with my cane in hand
I gaze across the sand,
As though within my reach
Spreads all that frames this beach.

My eyes were given me
To watch this tumbling sea
And thus to exercise
Most grandly with the eyes.

Then should I end up blind
All this will fill my mind,
Plus sights of those endeared
For whom I feared.

Or should my hearing go
I'll listen even so
To all that memory saves
Of voices and of waves.

Thus I'll be holding up
While I am folding up,
Somehow to shade away
Like dawn into day.

STAIRCASE AS RENEWAL

Was it start of spring or autumn,
An advancement down or up?
Switch above to light the bottom,
Switch below to light the top?

What implied? What consummating,
Moving thus from ground to ground?
Was it movement—or but waiting?
Was it fun—or misery-bound?

Was it like on tropic jewel-coast,
Leaving for sea or inland there?
Or by a solitary newel post
Standing, about to take the stair ... ?

(Let's admit it: I got into this one, in trying to sneak the
word "renewal" enigmatically into the penultimate line.)

DEMISE WHILE DESCENDING

> "If a man dropped dead while walking
> down stairs, he'd keep right on going."
>
> —Ancient Lore

A boisterous fellow, bubbly as a brew,
As bright as sunlight, and as genuine,
Where he waxed vocal, there the breezes blew,
All came alive when he came swinging in.

No colt or cub or pup could be more frisky,
He was a man of hustle, rustle, bustle.
Decisions to be made? He made them briskly.
With him, to laugh was a display of muscle.

He did not hear, it took him unawares,
The last time he went clattering down the stairs.

THE SCENE BEHIND THE SCENE
Mystique of a Drunken Word-Man

How can men help but misconceive
When hearts are worn upon the sleeve
Yet outward senses, duplicate within,
Are but a passage to their nether twin?

In the attempt to get things true
Poets confess to things they did not do,
And reproduce the dutiful
In clamoring for the beautiful.

The worm of living death,
Digestive tract with trimmings,
Expends its evolutionary breath
In exhortations, oaths, and hymnings.

How far from where men daily dwell
To that rare realm within the body's shell,
The scene-behind-the-scene's unseen frontier
And sounds like touch beyond the inner ear?

Up from the depths of secret utterance
(The innerness beneath each vital thing)
Into a trance of dance and chance
Standing on tiptoe in a tide's upswing

Words rise unbidden
Calling to and from the hidden
The verbal engine throbs ahead full throttle
While sick old age returns to nurse the bottle.

Already will-less as the dead
Except to swill while words get said,
Merging of east and west and north and south
The serpent-circle joining tail and mouth—

The sea sinks into oneness with its ships
And universal Love would kiss its own orating lips.

LINES FOUND IN A BOTTLE

"Dear Friends, and Gentle Hearts"
—words found on Stephen Foster,
who died dead drunk

Dear friends, and gentle hearts
Dear hearts, and gentle friends
Far away way down done gone
Dear strangers all my life
Dear strangers all to one another
Swanee me you'll find now movin' on.

EPIGRAM FOR EPITAPH

He had a lotta fun that day
Until, about to fall apart,
Trembling he went to pray
In the church of the scared heart.

LINES FOR A DEVOTION,
IN AN AGE OF SCIENCE

Almighty God, the world is full of fear
And all the world has trickled into me.

We must be ready to be done or done to, hear
Me, great God, with all Thy charity.

Careen now speeding to replace Career,
My God, I humbly beg Thee—*be*.

LINES FOR A DEVOTION

My tailors have failed me
My voice records badly
My mirror slanders me
My friends cannot get my jokes

O Lord
All around me
There is incompetence

I am thine,
To make of me as thou willst

ON IMPROVISING

It does not matter, God, to thee,
That a man would or would not concede thy existence.

It does not matter, God, to thee,
That he avoids thy Churches.

It does not matter, God, to thee,
That he is not theist or deist or any such.

It does not matter, God, to thee,
That he believes not one word of theologians' dogma.

But to him it matters gravely
If he falls to praising

And beseeching with lamentations
Far into the night . . .

ON DELAYING TO PHONE THE HOSPITAL

And if I do not call, not ever,
What might that mean?
We'll feed his dog.

   (Some dingy outfit in some far-off spot
Is vibrant with a prophet? Give the bloke
A girl, then blast the works to hell.)

Happy are those who can die in their own way.
Let me be gone quick
While batting at the piano like swear-words.

Of course you're guilty
When someone is sicker than you.

But who hasn't already written himself off?

HYPOTHETICAL CASE

Suppose you called into the darkness
Or across a valley at midday
Or through the woods
Or down a corridor, for that matter—
And got your answer.
Then what?

Suppose you loved clamorously,
Coupled,
Multiplied and prospered.
Then what?

Suppose you had fun,
Good friends,
Did public good,
Were fawned on,
Felt fine.
Then what?

Suppose you lasted long enough
To have plenty of occasions
To think much of death, disease, decay ...

IN MOODY COMMEMORATION OF A
SPIRITED JEWESS slated to die soon of terminal cancer

Tyrannous former student of mine
(two decades past and more)
There I was, on the rack,
even then—

Yet somehow here I'm still thrashing about
Towards a Next Phase
(terminal, to be sure, but less brutally, specifically so)

Poor Witch of Salem!
I cannot send you
this truest testimony of my
temporarily advantaged, deepest sorrow

Preparing to part for good
I wish you well

GLIMPSE OF GRANDEUR

By the road, a rabbit
"   "   "   , some weeds
"   "   "   , a gas station

On the road, traffic
"   "   "   , a traffic cop
And me—

All trying
To make a living

DISTINGUISHED COMPANY

Who am I, then,
Me saying these here words?
Whom am I saying at,
Across what bridge from what?

Insomniac words
From the wordless sleeping worm
Bringing gut conditions
Into utterance
Out of night-watch

Except me and the devil
Only God must stay awake so much,
Waiting
For all calls

A BATCH OF SELVES

All through the night
the music-makers

with their noises
went on asserting:

> *talk talkety talk talk*
> *talkety talk blank talk*

And all the while the dancers
signaled:

> *look*
> *see*

The whole works adding up:

> *me you us ours*
> *me me*
> *mine mine mine*

VIGIL

I've heard the whip-poor-will at dawn,
The hoot-owl in the night,
Heard dogs a-prowl across the lawn
And toms about to fight.

I've heard things getting ready
In their peculiar ways,
While time kept up its steady
Ticking phase by phase.

Waiting I heard
World without word.

AND HERE I AM, FIGHTING DANDELIONS

It's not their bright yellow
more frank than boastful.

Yet, though hurried and harried
careering and careening
I fare forth
to cut down dandelions.

I patrol the lawn, resenting how they spread
like a foreign policy.

At times I catch one *in flagrante delicto*
(in fragrant delight?)
in an orgy of miscegenation with a bee,
without benefit of clergy.

I dig up dandelions
at the height of their excesses.

(I fight fair.
No chemicals.
I'm a Rachel Carson man
and Organic Gardening—
and damn the fluoridation racket.)

Word goes forth:
"Burke's after us.
Hurry, proliferate,
be a population explosion."

From away back
the nice old lady next door
friendly to all
yet hypnotized by the *mores*

She raged against the Eyetalians
who swept across the grass in springtime
harvesting the honest dandelion

She fumed because they dug holes in her lawn— .
or was she but responding
to the way they crouched at their work
(stoop labor)
and hurried like stage criminals,
disappearing around the corner of Friendship Avenue?

HEAVY, HEAVY—WHAT HANGS OVER?

At eighty
reading lines
he wrote at twenty

The storm now past

A gust in the big tree
splatters raindrops
on the roof

Kenneth Burke

ON A PHOTO OF HIMSELF WHEN YOUNG

I musta had zipp and zingg in those days,
I'd call that Burke perky.

O'er forty years ago—
Yet even then
My heart was my pet canary

(how it hopped and twittered,
and kept the cage swaying)

It's still very much with me
As problematical as ever
Until the day (or night!)
When all controversy
Endeth.

Meanwhile me,
A vile old man,
Inclined to an old man's greed,
Seeing the seamy side,
Powerlessly exclaiming

Bring on your bombs, your bugs, and the trick chemicals,
Get this damned business done

But in the interim
Curse me for a not-yet-housebroken cur
And rub my nose in filthy lucre.

SELF-PORTRAIT

Cursed with a cussèd Ucs,
an unconscionable Cs,
and a pernicious Pcs

Besides the ills of
σῶμα, ψυχή, and πνεῦμα,
laden with the leaden burden of σέλφ

Gray and greasy grampa,
ole rattle-teeth,
something washed up on the beach

His frown not in anger,
but a rebound
from trying too hard to grin

No former Leftist sell-out to the Right
No Negro junky pushing for a white
No wonderboy whose chin is Beatnik-hairy
No o'er-ripe neo-ritualizing fairy—
Merely the average (lower middle class)
whom life keeps kicking gently in the ass.

None but a divorcee
who took a second try
A quite lop-sided me
with one lop-sided eye
A crooked ear, a crooked smile
and aims to walk his not too crooked mile.

KNOW THYSELF

(Mr. Stanley Edgar Hyman, Diagnostician, has written that "Burke has no field, unless it be Burkology.")

Here is a rarity
Brings no premium:
A Neo-Stoic
Agro-Bohemian.

One-third insomnia
One-third art
One-third The Man
With the Cardiac Heart.

When I itch
It's not from fleas,
But from a bad case
Of Burke's Disease.

What then in sum
Bedevils me?
I'm flunking my Required Course
In Advanced Burkology.

NOW I LAY ME

Insomniac, the poet is
hounded by currish doggerel

I would dally with sleep,
Would give slumber a tumble;
Would fall, even leap
Into somnolent rumble.

Should I tap a nightcap?
Sip a nip for a nap?
Try a stiff snort of booze?
Belt a snifter to snooze?

Too lethargic to rouse
From a drift into drowse,
In the arms of repose
May I dawdle and doze,

With a berceuse by Orpheus,
Cradled by Morpheus,
Making the best o'
A lengthy siesta.

All the nodding I do
Is for yes and for no.
So I reach with a will
For my pitiful pill.

ON THE REFLEXIVE

I woke and found that I was fighting
in ways that bring no power-or-pelf
while by a kind of anti-praying
somewhere a kind of voice was saying
"Only what writes itself is worth the writing."

But Anti-Echo answered, biting
"What only writes its Selph
Let it go read its Selph."

The work continuing,
"You are a blunder dunderhead"
it then went on and said,
"a technologic sin.

"Of all the self-denial gents
among whom hopelessly you are,
in earlier eras you'd have been
even against the violence
of our own Revolutionary War."

To meet the ravages of the reflexive
(as in "I hurt myself") I grant I'm ineffective
despite my great enjoyment of invective.

What's then to do but keep a-inchin' along
a millimeter at a time,
clinging to the shreds of song
until our scientists too greatly change the clime?

To somehow try to go on learning
to salivate the more and whimper less
and may
(in all this much-ado)
enough tomorrowness
keep turning
up to see me through
another day ...

PERSONALITY PROBLEM

I'm a teacher in a girls' school
And I don't want to fight,
But just outside my bedroom there's
A rooster crows all night.

At any part of any hour
He'll trumpet forth full swing.
He crowed in darkest winter-time,
And now bejeez it's spring.

He's in a solitary coop
From which his protests spout.
The wires that keep him from his hens
Can't keep the season out.

He's pent up with his hungers,
Frustrate in his career.
That's how to deal with people,
Not a chanticleer.

His virtues are not given vent,
His talents not employed.
He either ought to have his wives
Or else a course in Freud.

A SPECIAL KIND OF GLASS

Alcoholically confessant
he told her of a dream
he had in childhood—
and though it never once recurred
had never left him.

Of a giant woman
with breasts like bunches of grapes
plus one enigmatic detail:
those swelling clusters
were

GLASS

Glass grapes, by God!
yet as hugely pendant as full udders,
"Grapes, yes," he said—
"But why glass grapes?"

In turn she asked him
(she was the Administrative Type)
"Were you a bottle baby?"

And bejeez he was!

Drink up!

PLAQUE FOR A KIND OF OUTDOOR HOUSE

YOU INTELLECTUAL TWIRP
YOU DIM-WIT STINKEROO
IF YOU WOULD GO A-SLUMMING
THEN SEE IGNATZ DE BURP
THE ONE GUY IN *WHO'S WHO*
WITH PARADISAL PLUMBING
(HE CALLS NEW YORK A SEWER,
A BABYLONIAN HOOR)

ON CREATIVE DYING: AN EXERCISE

To speak at all is to be a tiny frog with a big voice. And if a frog can believe in himself—as he apparently does when twanging his fiddle in the marshlands—why not I? The difference is that the frog knows nothing of the news. Yet how can man know no news?

> Always that thought pursues:
> "How can man know no news?"

Poetry having been invented long before journalism, the ancient bards shrewdly became the first newsmen. In their travels they brought timely tidings (astutely edited) to exchange for bed and board. Then gradually things piled up, until now there's so much organized information assailing us, from all quarters, about human jeopardy in the large, how have they the effrontery to be any less impersonal than a tabloid headline?

THREE KILLED
IN CRIME WAVE

it said, thereby implying that those three particular endings were important mainly by reason of their place in a trend.

(I got a place in a trend. I'm better than him. My Ism is better than his Ism. True, I weep my heart out. But I'll glow like a blowed-on coal if you tell me I wept well. And anyhow, any mood, no matter how fleeting, is in its way pretty damned eternal, at least as long as there are people around. I got a place in a trend. You got a place in a trend. All God's children got a place in a trend. When I get to heaven I'm goin' to take out my place in a trend, I'm goin' to trundle all over God's heaven.)

Maybe the problem is along these lines: Particularly in this run-down post-Whitman era, few can versifyingly CONFESS in ways that build up the Poetic Image (to match the bureaucratic need for a National Image such as might be dreamed up by an expert Public Relations Counsel). Indications are that poets will fare best if their offerings are Plush, in a quasi-democratic sorta way. I hate, I hate, I hate. (Kill, kill, kill, kill, kill.)

Here is an Early Memory (not too early). It concerned a story about travelling across a desert. If the thirsting man came to a crystal-clear waterhole, he knew to shove on, sans to touch a drop. But if it was mucky and slimy, he knew that here was a liquid he could sop up in confidence. The glass-like clear one should be avoided, because it was poison, pure alkali. The mucky one was safe because, if all that other stuff could thrive there, then surely the human organism might commune with its nature. Think of that story as a PARABLE, when you buy modernique "processed" fruits and vegetables. Are they perhaps sans blemish simply because they are loaded with pesticides? A self-respecting worm would not be found in such a joint? Demand a runty, scaly, disfigured apple.

(How build up a viable Poetic Image, unless we can get togidda in avowing: Not one single apple, though it came from the Garden of Eden, unless it has scales and worms and general health-giving discoloration—in defiance of modernique sales promotion?)

This note came in, from a correspondent who was trying to reduce, and who, as regards modernique modes of obliteration, was disgrunt:

Our physicists are wonders all
And the bomb they made is a heller.
If only instead
Their prowess had led
To inventing a no-cal alcohol
I believe I could even stand Teller.

And who would deny that that's quite a lot of standing?

A decent man's job is, among other things, to grieve for his particular country's imperialism. He should leave it for the decent citizens of other countries to grieve for theirs. Guard against the goad to be self-righteous by being one's foreign neighbor's conscience's keeper.

Don't put your money in a hole in the ground. Put it in a savings bank where, if our politicians can contrive to keep things pretty much as they are, your sums will earn in interest just about the amt. you lose annually by Creeping Capitalist Inflation. The savings bank can use your deposits to make profits in ways that help cause this same inflation. But, like a good mediævalist, you won't be guilty of usury (*nummus nummum non parit*). Yet you won't lose out cruelly as though, like a mediæval miser, you had put your money in a hole in the ground. For that sorta thing had to do with when the tiny hoard was, like silence, *golden*.

I know what gives. Things filter down to the Great Three Stages at the basis of all human culture: (Latin) *puer, vir, senex;* (Greek) *pais, anēr, gerōn.* That is to say, from child to man to oldster—the first stage too young to bear arms, the second arms-bearing (plus all the qualifications and reservations!), the third blessedly too old. (I ptikly admired the attitude of a bright lad who, enrolled in training for the kill, loved to prove himself a good marksman in the absolute, while not even wanting to shoot a woodchuck. He was sorry for any poor duffers trying to make an honest living.)

Another correspondent sent in anonymously this disturbing statement (we tried hurriedly to locate him, but Intelligence fell down):

> I killed him while he sat at the piano. He died with his foot on the pedal, a shriek continuing for some time after. And the memory of the echo is still quick within me.

Yes, Intelligence fell down. The Poet's Image was slipping. He had no plush-carpet sentiments to encourage govt.-subsidized distribution overseas. Sans Eleganz. The best he might hope for was to be an arrested adolescent who managed not to get arrested. He kept thinking of the rich woman, who threw the leftover roast into the garbage. (The rich bitch, who kept her husband slaving to keep up.) He liked the idea of honeysuckle by the outhouse (suggesting as it did the nearness of motives sexual and fecal). And he despaired of the clean-cut, riding smooth-shod over sales resistance. Their spoiled brats would be like horses in a barn, eating all you'd give them, and doing nothing useful but shit.

"Scat! Cats! I've never met an ILGWU, no, not one." Yet he must have had a hang-over. For the windshield wiper kept flicking "Strep throat—strep throat." And when the wife said "messy edges,"

> "Messy edges" rang like "Snookie Ookums"—
> And "Snookie Ookums" just like "Essie Omo"—

behind the which disguise
there lurked a girl now possibly in heaven
whom he had known explorer-wise
when he was circa ætat. seven.

I would not fight with whom. I would not, nor for any-
thing, how that the day be sweet. If I were gracile enough,
I'd do an ironic idyll about a milkmaid with milkpail and
Geiger counter. Or a conceit about Sebastian, the patron
saint of fairies, pierced placidly with arrows. Or about a pious
penniless poet who named his children Iamb, Trochee, Dac-
tyl, Anapaest, and Spondee, since they were all born of
Rhythm. I'd keep on the go. To the best of my ability, all
would be hit and run in the transport department. I'd aver
as to how, in all decency, an undertaker should not violate
a corpse, lest he lose his license. And I've never met an
ILGWU, in either day nor night. Scat! Cats! And may God
give us a good groove in which to grovel. I once heard tell
of an Oriental potentate who, obsessed by fantasies of *vagina
dentata,* on the advice of the court magician was cured by
having all his concubines' teeth pulled. He put his money
in a Swiss bank, since the Swiss had been FREE for one hell
of a long time. And now he's on the Riviera, all set to stay
cleared out for good, as soon as Western subsidies can't any
longer stave off that much-needed revolution back home.

Quick! Close the windows. The lovely quickie storm has
let loose upon us. Let loose in ways compulsive to be pious.
(Afterwards I looked up,/ and there was that/ poor old/
run-down/ chopped-up/ but still there/ third-quarter/
Moon.) Pray think of me as a friendly fellow who would
make you feel at home by just sittn around complainin about

being bequeathed by the centuries an almost irresistible need to be a failure. (How believe in the saga "from canal boy to President" when there are so few canals?)

What's it all about? I'll tell you. I had thought of looking up a place I'd been forty years ago. I didn't know why, except that, when I was there then, I was more itchy with a Sense of the Unfulfilled than a dirty dog has fleas. So I said let's go back and see what the hell. That's not much of an Image. But it's a scientific fack, involving puzzles about occupations and destinations.

> What if it turned out that one's occupation
> Was but to have a wavering destination
> To each day keep on going on renewing
> Whatever it befell one to be doing?

We went by car, the wife and I (she putting up with this damned nonsense, while we drove and drove).

> As for the light that might explain,
> Oh, do you have the lamp, sir?
> This morning we were north in Maine
> We're now in south New Hampshire.

> We're here all set up for the night
> In a model motel, the price was right.
> And at no extra cost
> We found what was not lost:
> A sickly sickle of a moon
> The merest silver slither
> That makes one ask oneself too soon

Where go from whence to whither?
(Feeling the need to be elegiast
He had gone forth to check up on his past.
But lest it all bewitch him
He took the missus with him.)

Lines written in a motel in New England in late August.

I heard the pigeons cooing
And on the principle of *lucus a non lucendo*
I thought of mine enemies.
But my bleat having bled
I shall back to bed
(Having taken a good slug
of the inspissate incipience of alcohol.)

Interlude: Notes on a Picture in Progress—
with regard to the trip, say how, again and again, going
around a bend in the road, coming upon a vista... then,
near the end of the trip, stopping to visit a painter friend...
coming into his studio... there, begad, there was the truly
startling vista... on that massive canvas, only a few feet
square... the rock, not meant to seem enormous as regards
the imitation of sheer size... but enormous in its emphatic
thereness... like a great growth... a cross between a rock
and an imaginary flower?... maybe a kind of signature?...
    and the many disparate birds, in all sorts of momentarily
summational postures... the silent, motionless flutter-buzz
... (action-painting is all to the good... but why not, like
this, use all the resources natural to painting?... why not?)
    aside: on the history outside the painting... drawings

that trace successive transformations of the rock, from a squat, oblonguish thing lying on its side, into an upwardness, a mounting like a mountain ... or the preparatory sketches for other items, each with corresponding modifications, and bits ultimately selected ... including tentative strategic plans for the action as a whole ...

above all, the history inside the painting ... for instance, a broken tree stump, and the fitting of it rhythmically to the climbing of the rock ... the undulant snow ... and the human comedy of the birds ... yet what could have happened to them? ... they are in transit from where to where? ...

alighting ... standing still or turning around ... being glum, or alert, or in sundry other ways preoccupied ... beginnings, turnings, subsidences ... many birds, they seemed like many more ... a thesaurus of postures ... an invasion of disparateness ... the twitter of many unrelated bird-notes ... embodying a principle of fragmentation, to play off against undulances and solidities ... yet not like fragments of a thing broken, for each was a totality ... yet are they not the fragmentation of a flock? ... for whereas we think of a flock as all one, we here thought of many disparate ones, each in an attitude of its own, each at some different moment of fulfillment ... (am I remembering wrong? or was not each oblivious of the others, wholly wrapped up within itself?) ...

Let's see, how many elements in all? ... first, startlingly, suddenly, as you walk into the room: the rock ... all about it, the worry of the birds variously busy ... the wave-like snow, with small bits of rock jutting forth here and there, doubtless a thematic transition between the birds and The Rock ... a broken tree that has three distinct moments:

(1) its toppled top (2) still connected with a bristling stump (3) by some tough, sinewy strands of the trunk. (Your eye keeps connecting back and forth along the strain of that sinew. That's major.) ... and sky—though at this stage it escapes me ... the treetop is subtilized by what I'd call the "principle of ramification" (here got literally by the tree's lean branches) ... and I'd want to see this as another kind of transition into the birds as a "principle of fragmentation" (though conveyed not by breakage but by the clutter—or convocation—of individual birds) ... I keep tinkering with some vague "terministic" kinship between "fragmentation" and "ramification."

Having looked at all sorts of horizons for several days, coming around bends in the road, I entered the room—and suddenly I saw not "out there," but IN. (Maybe this accidental contrast explains why I'm vague about the sky) ... despite the almost documentary accurateness of the *things,* despite the ample evidence, both in the painting and in the preparatory drawings, that every stroke of the brush, while calligraphic, was also weighed against the objectivity of the object, here was an opening of another sort, an opening IN-WARD. It had to do with that keen paradox whereby, the more scrupulous the observations "out there," the more likely the disclosures are to betoken an *intrinsic* lurking ... Realism, sub, super, intra ...

Notes on a painting by Pierre Fleur, Rock Flower, Peter Blume ... that was a glowing interlude—that which I saw that time, though not coming around a bend ... yet it keeps on being there suddenly ...

End of interlude

Where were we? I was talking of a trip, vaguely in search of a vista, but with sights along the way. "Why hang on and on, like a chronic illness?" I asked in effect. "The glancing blow." ... "Be by twinges." ... "Call it pound, call it ounce —or pounce." ... "Or in terms of transport, hit-and-run." ... But what do about Image Trouble? Find somehow the sort of Poetic Selph competent to deal appropriately with governors of states who encourage the sort of thing that leads to the bombing of little children at Sunday School? Or else have no Poetic Selph at all—just Image Trouble? Or relegate some utterances to prose, some to verse, each assigned to a different aspect of the personality? My bleat having bled, I shall back to bed.

Somatics

"After forty, it's patch, patch, patch."

—Old surgical saw

Though it but sits and thinks
Even then it's shoddy.
How might I fool this jinx
My unheroic body?

A HUGE TRIBUTE

He had mighty bulges
This poet,
With vigor of movement.

His output was substantial.

When he swished
By God he swished—
And better keep your distance.

Magnitude?
Solemnity?
Poise?
Calm self-affirmation?
This one had them all—
And curvature.

I mean
He was a horse's ass.

I AM TOREADOR

Matador Self-Adore Bullshido El Conquistador
world-famous Spanish butcher
idol of the bull ring.

At the thought of me
Hemingway pissed his pants
with envy.

Girls pile up
They come faster
than they can go.

I torture
animals
with perfect elegance.

ART AND THE GOSSIP NOVEL

If he could write a vulgar dance tune
That went over big,
With a title that made it the theme song
For a vulgar movie that packed them in

A mixture of vulgar tear-jerking
And vulgar violence
And vulgar sex—
And he got a drag from that too

Then with all that cush
He could be pretty damned eleganz

Could buy a swankeroo place on some stinking classy beach
And have vulgar swankeroo eleganz booze-parties

And, all told,
Live like the critics
Admire F. Scott Fitzgerald for.

AN AUTHOR'S VISION OF THE AFTERLIFE
An Intra-Mural Poem

In those Great Days of Perfect Timelessness
When all will be like one long happy fart
Some swillin supernatural Scotch
Some boltin beatified bourbon
Some guzzlin rye
Some layin the ladies all over the lot
Some just catchin up on their heavenly homework
Some smitin their enemy's other cheek
Some comin
Some goin
Some just sittin there praisin
Some sellin dear
Some buyin dead cheap
At the ultimate auction
Eternally

And no one in hell at all
But Myron Boardman* of Prentice-Hall

---

* "Myron L. Boardman, who retired in 1963 as president of the Prentice-Hall trade book division (*PW*, October 7, 1963), has been elected to the board of directors of Hawthorn Books. Since his retirement from Prentice-Hall, Mr. Boardman has been executive director of the Foundation for Christian Living, which publishes and distributes the printed sermons and specialized writings of Dr. Norman Vincent Peale."—*Publishers' Weekly*, vol. 192, no. 16 (October 16, 1967), 42.

THE HABIT OF IMPERFECT RHYMING

Lips now rhyme with slops
Hips with blobs
Passion with nuclear fission
And beauty with shoddy.
The word for lovely leisure, "school,"
Is now in line with urban sprawl.
Are we blunted or haunted?
Is last year's auto a dodo?
Let widow be bedded
With shadow and meadow.*

All this is necessary
Says the secretary—
Else moan, groan, bone must go with alone,
As breath must go with death.

---

* As far back as high school, I decided that widow-shadow-meadow are the most perfect possible imperfect rhymes. Ever since then, I have been trying to fit them just right into a poem—and maybe some day I'll succeed.

TWO SPHINXES

I

Were I the sort, and would that I were that,
In coming to be near the place of start
While loving each appropriated art
And looking ever towards the goal whereat;

Were I the sort that when the times begin
In hoping what the trustfulness allows
And kneeling how Obeisance meekly bows
Throughout the steady progress towards the In;

Were I by all that circumscribéd were
With giving forth and bland receiving blest,
To answer each requital with behest
Despite the turn towards rightnesses that err,

Then would I ever ever want to be
All that The Message whispereth to me.

II

I would not give nor anything
How that the day be sweet,
Ask only of each darkening
That we be there to meet
        As were a paraclete
        Through journeying.

I would not ask of human ear
That such be of a form,
Nor turn about as though to hear
From norm unto abnorm
    As were the distant storm
    Forever near.

But I would ask of thee
Through every solemn task eternally

Relax, dear Reader. You'll never figure these out. For there's
nothing to figure, unless it's worthwhile trying to decide why
I enjoyed writing such nonsense in the first place. In any case,
they have proved their scientific value. I sent the Shakespear-
ean sonnet to a bright poet-and-critic friend, and got back a
vicious, serious answer. He had discovered what he mistook
for dirty personal references to himself, and was outraged.
Contemporary criticism has attained such competence, it can
crack any code, if only the enigma is in verse. On another
occasion I read the second exhibit to a friendly liberal lady
who promptly confessed that she had always had trouble
with poetry. To be "vatic" by these rules, the lines must be
quite disconnected in sense yet strictly connected in sound
(rhyme and rhythm), with all the parts *as though* senten-
tiously developing one sustained and solemn standard theme.

REACTIONARY FABLE

Thoth taught the birds to write. So every dawn
Was silently a-stir with craftsmanship.
All busily engaged in jotting down
New note-formations bird-dom might enjoy
At concerts at some future festival.

It gave to pause—and savants of the tribe
Kept check on each advance in theory
While brilliant youngsters barely off the nest
Worked out such possibilities in sound
As feathered flocks had never known before.

In theoretic silence progress reigned.
With each new season of developments
Came further conquests in the realm of tone,
While crows wrote music for the larks to sing
And larks set melodies for choirs of crows.

However long this era might obtain,
Some wished the birds would simply sing again.

A-E-I-O-U

The Word is a snare,
It lurks as in a lare.

The Word is a sneer.
It jeers as with a leer.

The Word can inspire,
It sings as with a lyre.

The Word is store and cure,
Study its lore and lure.

WORD-MOUTHINGS

Mrs. Orlando
Part-time Sappho
Swimmin with the women
Given to the crest of the wave
Asking only that the tiptoe moment
Flash absolute
That all be always
A just-about-to-be
Thinking of all else
In terms of its nearness from, or distance to
Such advenient abnorm

And Demosthenes
Learning to harangue the waves
By spouting with stones in his mouth—
What kind of twist was that?

THE BANSHEE GIRLS

A northwind blew around the
corner of the house, blowing
leaves down the road riotously.
Here is what blew in.

The banshee girls are howling,
The world is full of wail.
Won't you go a little slower?
Time is treading on my tail.

Oh, pearls are made for swine
And swine are made for pearls
And I have heard the whine
Of the banshee girls.

Though I am getting balder
The world is in my hair.
How can I help but falter,
With portents everywhere?

The nadir's at the zenith,
The wind is in the lee.
Let thine be mine but not mine thine
To all eternity.

Won't you go a little slower?
Time is treading on my tail?
The banshee girls are howling,
And the world is full of wail.

BIG CLAUS AND LITTLE CLAUS

"Giddyap, all my horses!"
Cried Little Claus,
Thus angering Big Claus,
Who had warned him.

For those horses, every one,
Were owned by Big Claus,
Little Claus's older brother
Who by mistake killed the Old Grandmother,
Who had been a drag on the family,
Eating the things
That otherwise
Would have gone to Little Claus.

Yet Little Claus had greatly loved her,
Even giving her his bed to sleep in,
Whereat Big Claus killed her by mistake,
Thinking to kill Little Claus,
But killing the Old Grandmother
That lay there in the dark,
In the bed of Little Claus,
Because Little Claus had been kind to her.

And so Big Claus was hanged as a bad man,
And Little Claus got the horses after all—
And put flowers on the Old Grandmother's grave.

This is a story
Thunk up by Little Claus.

THEORY OF ART*

You must illustrate and decorate and doodle
You must illustrate and decorate and doodle
Your work's not really done
Till you've got all three in one
You must illustrate and decorate and doodle

You must operate to get this through your noodle
To be perfect you must have the whole kaboodle
Not just one or two, by Gee
It requires the whole damned three
You must illustrate and decorate and doodle

---

*I'll hold to this absolutely if you'll but concede that, to a person of even sluggish imagination, forms no matter how arbitrary can suggest natural forms or fragments of natural forms; and that tricks of "uglification" can fall under the head of "decoration."

HE WAS A SINCERE, ETC.

He was a sincere but friendly Presbyterian—and so

If he was talking to a Presbyterian,
He was for Presbyterianism.

If he was talking to a Lutheran,
He was for Protestantism.

If he was talking to a Catholic,
He was for Christianity.

If he was talking to a Jew,
He was for God.

If he was talking to a theosophist,
He was for religion.

If he was talking to an agnostic,
He was for scientific caution.

If he was talking to an atheist,
He was for mankind.

And if he was talking to a socialist, communist, labor
        leader, missiles expert, or businessman,
He was for
        PROGRESS.

LINES ANENT AN INQUIRY

A loner in the Lone Star State
Where he was resident

A loner in the Lone Star State
He shot our President?

A loner in the Lone Star State
We know of his defections

But who is likely to relate
Just what were his connections?

RECITATION, FOR JAMES DURANTE, ESQ.

I said I like that
She said you like what
I said I like what you're doing
She said what am I doing
I said you know
She said you know what
I said no, what
She said yes
I said no get
She said get all gone
I said nuttin.

I said about whosis
She said which whosis
I said pick one
She said yes
I said he swipes
She said of course he swipes
I said what's that got to do
She said why not
I said every time he's been here I find something gone
She said why kick if you find it
I said what do you mean find it
She said that's what you said
I said nuttin.

I said I'd like to have some
She said you'd like to have some what
I said some whatever you got
She said you can have some any time you want
I said I'd like to have some now
She said she don't have any now
I said nuttin.

She said aw go pick berries
I said I don't know how
She said it aint like playing the piano
I said I can't play the piano
She said I mean you don't have to learn
I said who don't have to learn to play the piano
She said that's what I mean
I said nuttin.

She said all you do is pinch them
I said you mean berries or ladies' behinds
She said don't get stale
I said I was being fresh
She said that's what I mean
I said nuttin.

MY GREAT-GRAMMA BRODIE

My Great-Gramma Brodie
Wouldn't let me say "G"
'Cause it meant a swear-word.

My Great-Gramma Brodie
Knew about
Heck, Holy Smokes, and Darn it.
She helped me clean them up, too.

My Great-Gramma Brodie
Taught me a lot
About Implications.

APOSTROPHES BEFORE DESISTING

O Emerson/ looking from within/ upon outside/ shined on by the eye of none other than/ Ralph Waldo.// O Twain/ apparently clemently but actually brutally/ cut in two.// O Hawthorne/ your scarlet Alpha/ proceeding backwards/ from an enigmatically cardinal/ Omega.// O Whitman/ Our country's most ecstatic/ Priest and Bard of politicalized Sex-ease/ and kindred conundrums.// O Sea-mammal-hunting Lordman/ Gothic Pierre/ Melville.// And Mrs. Murphy/ whose boarding house/ improvising like Mom used to do/ is now found/ darkly threatened

Yours for guilt ascending or descending/ from beginnings.// The guilt of self/ a hand/ or the manifesto of a fist.// The guilt of/ the frozen essence of/ the fallen angelism of / Lovelessness.

All my life/ Scared by a sacred secret/ I've lived on the fringes/ an Ist Among the Isms./ I've been my own disease./ (In happier days/ Self-Reliance)

O let me be as much of a disgrace/ as I can risk/ and still pay the taxes./ Let me fall afoul/ but not too much/ of every specialty

I call hello-goodbye to all of you/ I ask what next/ Thus with appropriate vowels and avowals/ I have averred.

(*Dies, until the next time*)

PORTRAIT OF A PROBLEMATIC PATRIOT

(aria da capo, with glosses by a man with glasses)

As free as the driven snow
with nowhere and/or everywhere
to go

(he is, in effect, stumped,
immobilized)

Hoping that things might sizzle
with a keen sizzlement
fresh from the sizzlery
in an *envergure* of wingspread

(so he dreams of a life excessively
the opposite)

Wondering what it feels like
to be a drop of water
when not all out by itself
but melted in among its fellows

(hoping to transcend the
damned ego even)

He called forth hearkenwise
to whomsoever
and whomsoever replied not a word.

(he is in principle for a
grand convocation, but it
doesn't convoke)

He said to the self:
"When pecking at notions
Be like swooping down for the kill."

(he imagines enterprise
in terms of considerable
dash on his part)

He said:
"If itchy with ambition,
be your own Harpy,
and tear at yourself till you're raw."

(or as a kind of self-
violence made heroic)

He recalled the time by the shore's edge
when lying awake perforce at night
he pitied the poor insomniac sea
out there thrashing in the dark full moonglow
back and forth gritting its teeth in the sand
its problems endlessly unsettled.

(and engenders
a corresponding
conceit by iden-
tification with
a sea similarly
troubled)

"Oh," he breathed,
"to be in a permanent I-Thou Relation
with the Id!"

(guided by famous dia-
lecticians, he finds for his
malaise a formula stated
in terms of highest gen-
erality)

He called to whomsoever:
"Come one, come all,
that I may be thy shepherd
(though sheep otherwise are raised
either to be fleeced
or for mutton)."
And whomsoever replied not a word.

(whereupon there still
lurks the chagrin of the
convocation that con-
vokes not)

He peered into the devices of the leadership
for lining up the readership
and pondered on the ways
of college campi

(yet he would study; and having
studied, teach)

His gospel was simple but compelling:
"Things positively are, or not.
Get going, till you get or you get got.
We learn by rote and live by rot.
And people seem inclined to itch a lot."

(looking for a cure,
he puts forth theatric
thoughts that are
themselves symptoms
of the disease)

Having been told that *contra* means "against"
and that from *contra*
come such possibilities of grandeur as
"my country,"
he sadly fervored:

(learning from the
lore of language)

"Dear my Country,
We must stay hard and close against Thee
Throughout all misadventuring.

(he undergoes a rev-
elation of the rela-
tion of his station to
his nation)

"Be moral fortress
Not imperial fightress
With arms botched and debauched."

(and in terms of a timely
topic, he refers to a moral
and/or political problem
which, until it gets re-
solved, throws him back
again to stanza one)

246

EVERY INCH A KINK

Through (crazy) traffic
We fled the (crazy) snow
And here we are
By a (crazy) storm-tossed southern sea.

We saw the sun set
In a (   ) scattering of (   ) torn clouds
(Then all night long
My dreams were a tangle
Of traffic-laden storm-tossed blizzard
Of guilt, hate, meanness, murder.)

Might all the universe be old and sick—
Man's reason raging,
As full of kinks
As (crazy old) King Lear?

PRINCIPLE OF INDIVIDUATION

Each a surface
trails into endlessness
of now, past, future

fronts on other surfaces
(they rub)

rain earth air fire and fifth essence
fear hate pity tears love
"kill kill kill kill kill"
(wonder? laughter?)

Each of us a continuum
of

rays by a lens
bent to a burning focus

(In the books
Each is So-and-so
Citizen and Taxpayer)

How deep the shared depths?

Over all mountain tops is rest
Ueber allen Gipfeln ist *Ruh'*
(which, a symbol-man admonishes,
turns out to be *hur*ry turned backwards)

Now get you gone . . .

AS THE CURTAIN RISES

> (To be shouted loudly, fortissimo con brio)

(As curtain rises, a siren shrieks)
First Citizen: Who are you?
Second Citizen: I am Second Citizen.
First Citizen: And who are *you?*
Second Citizen: I am otherwise known as First Citizen.
First Citizen: There's something wrong here.
Third Citizen: As the curtain rose, a Siren shrieked.
Fourth Citizen: What do they want?
Voice: THEY WANT FULFILLMENT.
All: That's what everybody wants.
Voice: The play is about FULFILLMENT.
> *(They hold up the word in big type. Noises, ad lib.)*

Voice: Act one, scene two.
Second Voice: Imagine people doing and saying things so that you get all sorts.
Voice: That's just what they do do.
Third Voice: So what? And if not why not?

Voice: Act one, scene three.
(Enter Impresario. He speaks): Enter Impresario, limping.
Voice: A guy just jumped off a bridge.
Impresario: He got FULFILLMENT.
> *(Holds up placard with the word on it.)*

Voice: Act one, scene three continued. A street scene in Venice.

As we was saying: FULFILLMENT.
Oh, Beauty, Beauty. Thy name is
Truth-Goodness-Expedience, Mentalillness.

May every single criteria
in every single media
increase thy many kudos.

Second Voice: If you don't mind, we should arouse
expectations.
Romeo: Why not? How about me, Romeo—out there after
Juliet. I'm so ashamed of myself.
Voice: Maybe the guy can't distinguish between love for his
sweetie and love for his mother.
First Voice: Can you?
Voice: Shut up.
Second Voice: You filth. Why can't you be elegant and
good-natured, like he and I?
First Voice: I guess they all want jobs.

Voice: Somebody must be pictured trying to get something.
Second Voice: And there must be interference.
Voice: That's all there is to it, except the development.

Romeo: They must build me up as a handsome young lover.
Juliet: And me as a pretty girl who would get tied to Romeo,
by a knot not yet untied.
Voice: It's surprising to learn that there are still some left.
Romeo: What I did to myself is nobody's business.
Juliet: What I did to myself is nobody's business.
Voice: This is to be a play about private enterprise.

Vox Prima: I knew a guy who stuffed his head into an oven and turned on the gas.

Vox Secunda: Then what?

V.P.: Somebody by mistake pulled him out before he was done.

Thirteenth Citizen: I get it! No FULFILLMENT.

    (*All hold it up, upside down.*)

    (*Interlude, including earthquake, plus corresponding Earthquake Love, and delirium tremens, from the bottom of my heart and the bottom of the bottle.*) (*A guy hurls his glass at the wall. Silence.*)

Voice: What are we after?

Second Voice: We must build up expectations.

All: We want jobs, but soft ones.

Second Voice: Expectations, and FULFILLMENT.

Voice: There's that damned word again.

Impresario: Frankly, I don't ... (I ain't sayin')

    But I know this much:

        a limp
        a squint
        a leer
        a smirk
        askew
        akimbo
        malinger
        sniff
        dodge

251

hunch
louche
slap-happy
chasm-conscious

There's character in traffic accidents.

(A Siren shrieks. But Ulysses can't hear it. His ears stuffed with having-lived, he's already home.) (Delayed Response: Sound of a glass smashing.)

Epilogue (spoken by 68th Citizen):
computer mentality
bulldozer mentality
wonder-drug mentality
space-man mentality
driving-as-though-driven
aged-while-you-wait
promoter mentality
pesticide mentality
detergent mentality
murderously-waxed-floors mentality
prowl-car mentality

I feel mirzable

Listen,
all you Shrewdies—
Buy Consolidated Overkill.

POETIC EXERCISE ON
THE SUBJECT OF DISGRUNTLEMENT

In the offing: "Holy, holy—
Anoint and sanctify."

About the edges:
"Pray, beseech, give alms, atone by suffering,
Penance and repentance.

"My fault,
My gravest fault,
My most momentous, impious, sinful moment."

Seek absolution
In the Absolute.

Aristotle: "There is cause for alarm
If either injustice or outraged virtue
Has power."

      *   *   *

Vengeance, retribution,
Imprecation, malediction—
"Lament, lament,
But may the good conquer."

Guilt through the doing of forbidden things,
Guilt by forbearing to do forbidden things—
And hope by grief to rid the self of grievances.

Estrangement, defilement, sacrifice,
Filth, evil,
Each idiot, with his special idiom.

I knew a man, well-heeled in sadness,
And you would be surprised.
A stinkeroo he was, and as a guide
Exceptionally dirty, a pestilence
In his offensiveness.

Victim, martyr, guilt, wereguilt,
Debt, redemption (that is, ransom from captivity),
Blood-feud, blood-guilt, sin-offering, blood-offering.

By "sin-eater" is meant "a man who (according to a
            former practice in England)
For a small gratuity ate a piece of bread
            laid on the chest of a dead person,
To take the sins of that dead person upon himself."

Brutus: "We shall be called purgers, not murderers"

Purification through the word, that casts out demons;
Purification by cleansing, by things ritually clean;
Purification by sacrifice, scapegoat:
"Without the shedding of blood,
            there is no remission of sins."

Let them be saved in celibacy, virginity, abstention;
Let them be washed with *gomez,* the urine of the sacred cow.

Suffering from a vile disease,
He hoped to cure himself by giving it to others.

      *   *   *

In general, a god preferred male victims;
A goddess, female,

"It was the custom at Athens
  To reserve certain worthless persons,
  Who in time of plague, famine, or like
         visitations from heaven,
  Were thrown into the sea, with fitting incantations,
  That the people might be purged of their pollution."

Above off-scourings (the refuse of a sacrifice)
There arose those Great Persecutional Words:
Justice, Right, Necessity, Reverence, and Fate.

O that was a most fertile Indo-European root
From which sprang crime, crisis, criticism, discrimination,
Sincere, and excrement.

Brunetière on drama:
"Struggle against fate, against the social order,
         against someone of like nature,
  Against oneself under duress,
  Against a background of ambitions,
         interests, prejudices, stupidity or
  Malice."

Still, says Racine,
"It is not necessary that there be blood and death in tragedy.
It is enough if the action have magnitude,
If the agents are heroic,
If the passions are aroused,
And if the whole is suffused
With that majestic sorrow
Which constitutes the tragic pleasure."

Classical dictionary:
"The performance of a tragedy
was generally made the occasion
for a great display
of spoils
of war."

And right out of Pierre Corneille (1608–1684)
I shouted key terms in Middle-Western French:

gloire   honneur   royaume   pouvoir   devoir
   admiration   honneur   justice   couronne   honneur
puissance   courage   triomphe   autorité   honneur

great deeds   noble rage   just punishment
   large-minded conquest   submission

quotes: "and in pitying my sorrow, admire my virtue."

Fires of torment in Hell
Purgatorial fires
Fires of lust

Fires of love
Protective rings of fire
Fire ultimate.

*   *   *

O Spirit of Tolerance, frailly crooked-smiling,
O loveliness,
Would I might be to Thee
What all were on the verge . . .

I would slough off
My slough.

We ask what time—
And common sense might say:

It's between five-thirty and fifteen minutes to six.

But poetry might say:

Between fight thwarted and fighting
Moans to sick.

We ask where to—
And common sense might say:

Straight down that road and turn right.

But poetry might say:

Straight to the right
Until you come
To L—L—E—Aitch
Spelled backwards.
Then turn inside upside down and out—
And you vermine,
I mean you depraved image of God,
You're
Home . . .

Poetry is an old wound
Again breaks open.
Poetry jams your face
Hard against the past.

(Spirit of Tolerance, frailly crooked-smiling,
Song is sweet
And filth is power—
And I love you.)

*   *   *

The fellow said
"Here is a-rope-
You-might-need-some-time."

He said,
"Here is an excellent poison,
It could come in handy."

He said,
"This is fool-proof, sure-fire,
THE END."

And I thanked him,
His clockface staring at me
Like the windows of someone else's house.

Even his jokes were grisly.
"Avoid alphabet soup," he said,
"Or think of all the dirty words
  You'll swallow."

He said,
"Love if you can.
If not love, cry if you can.
If not cry,
Kill if you can."

A time of bated breath,
Apocalypse, and rabies—
Power over universal life and death
Now in the hands of babies.

(Power loose in feeble fists)

    *   *   *

Frankilee, O frankilee,
Mankind is a-thirst for new-things
Statistically predictable.

Frankilee, O frankilee,
The times are like a swamp
Frantic with mosquitoes.

The presses clack of calamity
Like a colloquy of crows.

I knew a woman as coldly designing
As spideress or former poetess.

I heard of Beauty
That fell like a thud of brick.

I knew an one as cold in her designs
As spideress or sour ex-poetess.

Frankilee, O frankilee,
How can you, having but one back,
Be backed against so many walls?

The single problem:
War and peace.
Not peace by devastation,
Not peace by enslavement,

Not peace by tax-collecting
Of imperial pacification,
Not peace that rots—
But peace,
Somehow.

Frankilee, O frankilee,
Frankilee, O frankilee,
There is a gorgeous canyon
Lifts up its naked gash
Towards a rainstorm fresh descending.

*   *   *

Spirit of Tolerance, frailly crooked-smiling,
Heal us with old age,
Comfort us with sorrow.

Meet me at the secret meeting place
Hid among the traffic.

Meet me near the lions
By the big library.

I have gray hair
Blue eyes
Glasses
And a mole under my right armpit.

They call me "Misery"
Because I love company.

And I am gloomy early of a wine-clear evening
While a slithery sliver of a silvery moon
Goes down nascently crescent.

Sleep, gentle sleep at eve,
That slides into the ravelled sleeve
And once again from pole to pole
Knits up, beloved, the careworn soul.

A COMEDIAN, ON HIS CALLING

I tried to do one thing, but by mistake did another.
It was terrific

I said "Mr." where you should say "Mrs."
That drove them wild

When I was told to pull out a chair for the lady
I pulled it out so she fell on the floor.
They nearly went crazy

I scratched funny-like
like a monkey with fleas.
They fairly howled

I made a face to show that my drink
Was a slug of alcohol.
A roar went up

I tried to drive a nail, but hit my finger instead.
They exploded

I got stuck in my own chewing gum
I made jokes about marriage

I stumbled over something I had put there
to trip somebody else

In acting like trying to swat a fly
I knocked over all sorts of things

It helps them get their mind off theirself

THE EARLY HOUR

Translated from Hermann Hesse: *Die Frühe Stunde*

Under a sheet of silver ["silver overflown"]
the field rests and is still,
a hunter lifts his weapon,
the woods roar, and a lark starts up.

The woods roar, and another ["a second"]
starts up, and falls.
A hunter lifts his plunder
And day steps into the world.

*

Silbern überflogen
ruhet das Feld und schweigt,
ein Jäger hebt seinen Bogen,
der Wald rauscht und eine Lerche steigt.

Der Wald rauscht und eine zweite
steigt auf, und fällt.
Ein Jäger hebt seine Beute,
und der Tag tritt in die Welt.

AMBULANDO SOLVITUR

An Exercise in Free Translation

It is solved
by walking

It is solved
by walking very very fast

It is solved
by walking out

It is solved
by the ambulance

It is solved
by the perambulator

It is solved
by a space-walk
query

It is solved
by talking back and forth
while going for a walk
together

EXTRADUCTION FROM WHAT?

There are our machines, our politics, and our selves. One cannot clearly distinguish the individual self from its merging into the collectivity, except in the sense that all our experiences necessarily have unique ways of being alike; and our physical pleasures or pains connot be *immediately* shared, no matter how sympathetic one person might happen to feel towards another.

Recently, having been asked to give three public talks, I had that simple design impressed upon me. So, for the first talk, I discussed the absurdity implicit in a driver's sense of power, whereas he is comparatively a weakling, and all the might is in the machine he happens to be driving. For the second talk I discussed the risks of political identification, whereby a man who may happen to be personally peaceful and unassuming can be obnoxious with boastfulness as regards his nation, which he feels should be the biggest bully since the start of time. Whereas he would despise a powerful man who mauled a frail one, he may positively gloat at the thought that his country, equipped with the ultimate resources of technology, can invade a small, technically backward people thousands of miles away, and in aiming to impress its will upon them can dump upon the backs of peasants such fabulous wealth of weaponry as was not even remotely possible in the previous wars of all history.

And for the third talk? Well, I happened now and then to have written some verses, variously related to my morbid Selph, lost among the monsters of machinery and politics, and hardly other than an insect which, while making tiny noises after the nature of his kind, could never know when some huge creature of the forest, heavy-footed as a mastodon, might just happen to stamp him out, merely in the course of going on its way. So, after having proffered some "Uneasy Thoughts on Automotive Man" and some equally uneasy comments on "The Responsibilities of National Greatness," for a wind up I tried a sampling of the items presented in this book. And I chose as title: "It's Good to Be Alive, or: Pardon Me For Living."

Since the vast Bureaucratization that is imposed upon us by the marvels of modern technology coexists with the threat of equally vast calamity, we can imagine two quite different responses. We might expect modes of expression designed to help us line up one another, for the better ordering of "global" traffic. Or there might be medicinally capricious refusals, at least in tentative moments, to abide by the rules at all. The obligations of traffic call forth attitudes as different as complete sobriety and driving while drunk.

Thus, at the very least, the "Lyric I" might conceivably swing between (1) such modes of utterance as Officialdom could distribute abroad, to help put a better light upon our not too imitation-worthy National Image, and (2) the "deviant" or "irresponsible" imitation of whatever moods a writer might have felt like.

Things are further complicated by the fact that, whereas a writer as citizen and taxpayer in some ways "identifies himself" with the momentary attitudes which he embodies as a lyrist, the union is by no means perfect. For instance, he may write some lines breathing total hatred of technology. Yet he may be quite aware that, insofar as the modern world is not being vexed by the spread of technology, it is languishing from the lack of technology. Or he may adapt, as though it were his very own, a notion that he picked up by sympathetically or antipathetically identifying himself with someone else. And while the general trend of such utterances is inexorably his, there is also a sense in which any "Lyric I" is a fiction, based on a deliberate willingness to see life unsteadily and to see it in parts, under "controlled" conditions specifically set by the terms of the given poem. In any case, the attitude will have the kind of wholeness that characterizes any attitude, however partial or partisan.

A writer may praise or lament or inveigh, for good objective reasons. But there may also be the technical or formal fact that he particularly enjoys the accents of praise or lamentation or invective. Thus he may seek to express such attitudes in their purity, whereas in "real life" they are usually cluttered with extrinsic matter, and so cannot attain for the reader the kind of "spontaneity" that a writer's revisions by commission and omission make possible.

Or the writer may happen to be also a critic who never feels quite right about criticism unless it is moderate in tone and at least theoretically charitable. Under such conditions there can be quite a gap between prose-patience and verse-patience, with the latter even looking more like verse-impatience. The very attempt to be circumspect in criticism could make one, by rebound, at least *wish* for *some* verse in the style of a news broadcast blasting forth pellets of info like a cashier punching money back at you through a change-spitter. Even the tonalities of rage are to be courted (especially if they retain enough of the infantile to be soon over, and as soon forgotten until the next time).

As for the several poems about dying: In the end they will necessarily be "proved" to have been "prophetic." Meanwhile, there are occasions when talk of dying helps one go on living. There is also the fact that the birth of new motives can be quite properly signalized as the death of old motives. The black, beady eyes of the chickadees (as per p. 294) do somehow seem to be looking out at one from an essentially different realm. And there lurks about, somehow, the Spenglerian equating of death with our current technological gigantics. In any case, having learned to tell time, we know that time will tell. But all told, alas! the general tenor here is anything but Plutarchian.

Later, another kind of postscript suggested itself. After having put the pieces in one order, I next decided that I should try rearranging them under various subheads. Here are some of the tentatives (I leave the list wholly at random, as it occurred to me):

> nostalgia
> stock-taking
> tinkering
> impatient
> on the last time
> frisky
> thrashing about
> bellyaching
> anecdotage
> editorializing
> good clean fun (that is, mildly doity)
> towards stentorianism (blustering)
> self-pity for others
> paranoid
> running scared

petulant
dwindling
enigmatizing
being complimentary
on the *Zeitgeist*
feeling mean
apprehensive
epistolating
pious

   As you will note, they overlap hopelessly, so that the same item could belong under several of such loose categories. In abandoning the project, I left things pretty much as they were, though a certain progression should make itself felt if the reader will follow the order here given.

   Many of the lines have never been submitted to the rigors of magazine publication. I felt that those particular pieces would profit best by a collective situation in which they might prop up one another (unless mine enemy might contend that they but drag one another down). In brief, among those poems that might propose to stand alone, there are others that might better be offered as paragraphs than as stanzas. But what's wrong with paragraphs, if they but help get it said?

K. B.

Tecate, California
March 1967

IN CONCLUSION

HOW HAD BEEN

I

Before then—
if want
we put words
they go
[*there had been postal service*]

II

Before then—
if want
we give   get
in big places
[*there had been supermarkets*]

III

Before then—
if want
all night
music
[*through broadcasting, around the clock*]

IV

Before then—
all not like
smashed-up now
[   ]

After awaking and writing these words (circa 3:30 A.M.), Our Hero went to sleep again, and dreamed a spectacular. A large sausage-shaped aircraft on fire, falls smoking to the ground. Soon after, a large box-like house (like an apartment house of about five or six stories) falls slowly out of the sky. Then several oblong skyscrapers, each larger than the preceding, fall slowly in much the same area, the heavily populated downtown section of a city.

These big buildings slowly toppled over, crushing the structures beneath them. Our Hero could see the great agitation, as people began attempts at escape and rescue, efforts interrupted by the descent and slow toppling of still larger structures. Though this calamity was but a short distance off, there were no sounds. The forms and movements of some victims seemed exceptionally distinct. While the dreamer was horrified by the situation, he also found it fascinating (perhaps like spectators witnessing a bad crack-up in an automobile race). He kept making observations to a silent companion of absolutely no identity, someone beyond the rim of his vision, to the left. And somehow, when referring to the disasters, he was also causing them to occur.

Doubtless, a "final" dream—an apocalyptic "vision of fulfillment," though in a bad sense. A dream of first and last things (by uniting the alpha of the style with the omega of the story). And, it seems to tie in with the dreamer's ineradicable conviction that there is an essentially *destructive* motive gnawing at the roots of technologism. All told, subsidence made "perfect"?

CASE HISTORY

Bored with

Build-ups
Smears
Bellyaches
Flatteries
Promises
Threats
Boasts
Confessions
Challenges
Controversies
Diagnoses
Dialogues
Catalogues
Details
Generalities
Market reports
Petitions
Protests
Prognostications
Questionnaires
Surveys
Digests
Outlines
Indictments
Insults
Inside info
Official hand-outs
Apologies

Things to show how delicate
Things to show how indelicate
Songs or anti-songs
Pomps and circumstance
People with their hair down
People with their pants down

Tweet-tweets
Yap-yaps
Klunk-klunks
Twat-twats
Buzzy-wuzzies
Ringy-dingies
and
Splotch

The poor baystard went out and looked across a field
he had cut with his putt-putt.
"Begad, jes look at that!" he said to his Selph—
Then Went Back
Into The House

TOSSING ON FLOODTIDES OF SINKERSHIP
A DIARISTIC FRAGMENT

I

the continent spanned eight times
major engagements in the Traffic War
lived through as with the soldier:
an otherwise lethal bullet
lodged in the pages of a Bible
next his heart
(in earlier days
when wars boasted less thorough
a science)—

he had put his all on Lucky Accident
the one sure winner
a whirlwind (when she runs)

in the Traffic War
that goes on like crazy
(each driver going somewhere, the whole thing nowhere)
we went north of the Great Lakes
crossing at Niagara
once a roar to pray by
now Pure Sewer
a Monster Spew—
"Surely," I told the Selph
"there's contamination even in the spray"
(I felt it on my lips, and spat).

But no—no self-respecting germ
would live in that filthy overflow
of POWER FOR PR*GR*SS

crossing the continent by car
finding marvels—and much desolation

leaving Canada at Sault Ste. Marie
Superior now to the north of us
already burdened with misuse
then over the plains to the mountains of Montana
and the glorious *Savings* in the Glacier park
then on to the Inroads of Destruction
in the Far Northwest

all the while driving with untoward thoughts:
"What if that oncomer veered into our lane?"
"What if a tire blew exactly now,
amidst this racing automotive tangle?"
(at times cars bunch up, moving along together,
like houses clustered in a village)
"What if, for no damned reason,
I gave a twist and sent us pitching
into that cataclysmic chasm,
that psychological gerundive,
that to-be-tumbled-into?"

meanwhile, the car plunging not down but forward,
there flows past our wheels
the ever-changing signature of empire,
proud, with its ruins

Why think so of the transitory?
because I am in transit?
quoting within me

> And on the pedestal these words appear:
> "My name is Ozymandias, king of kings:
> Look on my works, ye Mighty, and despair!"
> Nothing beside remains. Round the decay
> Of that colossal wreck, boundless and bare
> The lone and level sands stretch far away.

Ruins and pride of empire
in peaceful coexistence—
ugliness and power
weeds struggling to make an honest living
in slag heaps, among iron skeletons,
machines dead in use or disuse
This is our gospel for all mankind?
This we will bring to Vietnam?
(Hell! we have power enough
to tear apart a dozen tiny Vietnams
and build them up again with junk—
we and the Russians
already with our litter on the moon)

> Forever alive, forever forward,
> Stately, solemn, sad, withdrawn, baffled, mad, turbulent,
>   feeble, dissatisfied,
> Desperate, proud, fond, sick, accepted by men, rejected
>   by men,
> They go! they go! I know that they go, but I know not
>   where they go,

But I know that they go toward the best—toward some-
   thing great.

I wonder . . .
Whitman whistling in the dark
your songs of open roads in sunlight
you couldn't have foreseen
the many-laned ones
graded and landscaped
sometimes through nowhere
(it sure took infloonce to nail them deals)—
But we must guard lest
with a foot lightly on the gas
marvels grow cheap

the speed-drugged driver
heading head-long towards a sort of destination
while cogitating aimlessly
his thoughts   go   go   go
always on the self-same spot
like gogogirls—

Out of Bismarck
while the motor strained on the northern prairies
a primal quietude opening up inside us
across the wheatfields of Montana
driving twice the distance of the day before
and ending up *relaxed*.
Am I intrinsically a plainsman?

Not quite:
on a mirror lake at Glacier

the mountains rising like fury
their peaks naked rock
but farther down wooded heavily
mostly by pines
on the steep slopes living dangerously—
we happy that for four days this would be our homeland
(*Ubi bene, ibi patria*)
—and we'd find few Americans, thank God,
the season being nearly over.

Here, with the memory of so much undoing
you stand in the sign of Conservation.
(On a trail, through woods,
there spread suddenly one of Nature's clearings,
a pond and meadow, circled by high trees
behind much higher peaks
downpointing in the water.
The mystery maybe
a reflex counterpart of all the plunder
that had been flowing
beneath our wheels)

After drinks, dinner—
in the quietude of evening
taking vague inventory of my mindlessness,
speed-emptied:

"Hurrying westward with a message,
soon now we'll be arriving.
What tell 'em when we get there?"

II

How walk faster, except by working harder?
Likewise how run, or speed up a bike,
except by greater effort? ...
Ever so lightly press the pedal down a fraction farther
And your massive technologic demon
spurts forward like a fiend.

Tell them that.
Talk of such brutal disproportion
between decision and the consequences.
"Might we not here, my friends,
confront the makings of a madness,
an unacknowledged leap
from *This is mine*
to *By God, this is ME!* ...?

Might our mechanic boastfulness
contain, in this quick easy magnifying of the self,
(to match industrial wastefulness)
a fatal moral canker?
Is it all over,
already at the start?"

Say what the traffic calls for
(I got it down to these)
    (1) A rudimentary aptitude
    to give and interpret signs

(2) Emergency-mindedness.
I'd call it "caution,"
but what truly cautious man
would drive at all?

(3) Considerable good luck.
(Recall that incident when
had you been but a car-length
farther ahead or back at that particular moment
you'd now be recalling nothing)

(4) Obedience to the rules—
especially hard
since cars, like guns,
are medicine for the ailing ego,
and who is not an ailing ego?
(What profit extra power
unless it's flaunted?)

(5) Though Whitman
apostrophizing ideal travellers
elatedly spurns "riches,"
it is but by the grace of money
that all the parts of travel
commune with one another.

Leave out money—
and no mightiest of tyrants
imposing his absolute will upon a subject people
could remotely match these bonds of service
that bind free men together.

Tied by this knot
strangers minister to strangers
in self-willed strife with one another
striving to give the best years of their lives
towards answering a motorist's demands
for fuel, food, lodging, repairs, and entertainment.
Add but this major comprehensive Virtue
and the vast network
falls into place as by an act of nature
like thirsty cattle leading themselves to water.

["Dear Baucis," said Philemon, "a motel is the thing.
The money we have saved up through these years,
let's put it into that.
We could take care of eight or ten rooms a night
without too great a strain.
Let's pick a likely spot, and buy or build there."
His plan pays off. They make out fairly well.
True, even the thoughtlessness of customers brings pain.
Things that should be pulled, they twist—
things that should be twisted, they first try abruptly pulling.
So there is a steady drain of minor technologic mayhem
to cut the earnest aging couple's income over outgo.
Nor is there a pair of wandering deities in disguise
to stop for the night unrecognized
and bless them for their hospitality.
Still, their efforts are rewarded;
the stream of custom is moderate but constant.
They're working off their debt.
Then, just as a restive river shifts its course,
so Progress on the highway takes a turn.

A by-pass (aided by infloonce)
cuts through the region at a distance,
leaving the neo-hostelry far from shore,
to be ignored, or found by penny-pinching Wandering
    Scholars,
in search of bargains,
though ready to weep in principle
at such victimage.]

Tell of such things as that?
And meanwhile
let it ride   let it ride   let it ride

III

Snatches of other trips, remembered piecemeal,
keep crowding in:

That time when,
crossing the desert in the heat of noon
with a full load
we whipped up our young mare unmercifully
and she never faltered
(Advt.   advt.   advt.   a Chevelle '64)

Crossing the desert west into Barstow
surely few better roads anywhere
and few meaner landscapes.
We arrived, to find the town avowing variously
"Who knows? Maybe it's true we loathe you.
But we revere your money. Welcome, welcome."

A bizarre bazaar—
no place ever beckoned harder
in all conceivable shapes and sizes and multi-colored
    blinkings,
signs everywhere of that awful Growth Disease.

Above the canyon at Yellowstone
after having taken in the sights all day
chasm-cringingly
I plunged all night
(on the edge of the abyss
clutching frail bushes
that tore loose at the roots)
up there, looking down

but at Zion, at the bottom of a canyon, looking up—
and all night I heard the deep convulsive intake of the desert
through the gulches.

In the Big Horns
around many a squirming, wriggling
squiggle-curve
after the obvious Presidential colossi at Rushmore
we saw, chiselled by nature out of cliffs above us,
pagodas, temples, ziggurats, columns, spires, archways,
deformed giants, apocalyptic beasts—
all of them works in progress
and merging profusely
into one another

Leaving Gila Bend
numerous saguaros

signalling
but what?
their shapes like Joshua trees
a cactus trying to be a yucca.
The driving was so easy,
though we started late
we came to the Canyon early
got a place but a few yards from a drop-off.
Shafts of slanting sunlight
struck peaks beneath blustery clouds.
Haste in unpacking
plus alcohol
plus aftermath of last night's sleepoes,
plus altitude—
all added up
to a flutter-heart.

To that great cataclysmic chasm
I doff my don.

The Badlands
as brightly colored as a baboon's behind
les mauvaises terres à traverser—
and the Grand Tetons
what an enormous sow
those Big Tits made of Mother Earth!

or the motel
where the mountain rose
right out of the backyard

or the Florida beach
so comically peopled by
Sweep-swoop Scoop-scum the Skimmer
Rusty-Hinge, the Gull
Line-up, the Tern
Hurry-hurry Hunchback Twinkle-legs, the Sanderling
Peck-peck Pink-beak Pink Feet, the Dove
Slow-go Pusho, the Terrapin
Deacon Double-life, the Pelican (an old witch when flying)
Patient scheming Handy-Paws, the Racoon (fussing at the
   garbage lid)
Up-down Up-down, the Porpoise
Blacksnake-neck, the Cormorant

or a stretch of beach on the Pacific
with kelp, shells, pebbles, oil slick
and a rusty empty can
of Chicken of the Sea.

and many more
O God our Law-Word
while the ship of state
sails grandly on through history
driven by a stiff breeze
from North-South-East-West

IV

What tell them?

"Perhaps the pollution at Niagara rates highest.

Just what befalls the psyches of initiates
on traditional pilgrimage
to celebrate their Fall
into that state of pre-divorce
better known as Matrimony?"

"I speak in my role as Wandering Scholar,
which is to say:
half experimental animal,
half control group.
I am mine own disease."

"Why shouldn't youths steal cars,
if property is theft
and cars are an aggrandizement?"

go   go   going West, the wife and I—
I told the Selph I'd say again
them resonant words of Horace Greeley,
"Go West, elderly couple."

driving   driving   driving
for shame! my Ideal Me a mediaeval Wandering Scholar
brought up to date Detroit-wise ...

"Might not the wide-spread ownership of cars
give all of us a sense of power enough
to need no other grumblings?
What with our private monster
mighty and responsive
might we incline to silence protests,
and go along with leaders?

Like Lawrence of Arabia
drive   drive   drive
to keep from thinking
of thousands and thousands battered
some thousands of miles away
that a mistaken outfit here on our Potomac
might somehow save its face?"
But hold! I couldn't tell them that!

All honor to Horne Tooke!
"Horne Tooke? Who was Horne Tooke?"
"A theorist of language who, in England,
got tried for treason, though without success,
for having had success in gathering funds
to aid the wives and children of the colonists
who fell at Lexington and Concord."
All honor to Horne Tooke!
And let us hope that history proves unjust
lest our great country suffer desolation
proportionate to that
now done by the squandering of our enormous treasure
upon the naked backs of peasants.

Great God our Law-Word, let history prove unjust . . .

Babylonian Towers everywhere—
Temples to a Trinity
of science, finance, and war.

Cook them with napalm in the name of freedom
tear up their way of life
herd them

let their girls get work as whores ...
then tell yourselves
how you can buy those people off
once you have loaded them with U.S. gadgets,
gifts from our technologic Christmas tree.

I can't speak for you, my friend,
but if that's what an invader from halfway round the world
with schemes for my deliverance
did for me and my ways,
I can't speak for you, my friend,
but with my country torn to pieces
by such expert squandering,
I can't speak for you, friend,
but I'd just bide my time ...

Gad! I couldn't tell them that!

Maybe I can't say anything ...
in our modern weapons there's about as much protection
as in eight simultaneous world-wide epidemics
seven major earthquakes
nine super-twisters
a dozen mighty tidal waves
nineteen volcanic eruptions as cataclysmic as Krakatao
and a collision with a comet
half the size of the moon

Go   go   go
let it ride   let it ride   let it ride
drive   drive   drive
but shrewdly, lest you be vowed to accident

like that compulsive speeder who
returning from Arabia
smashed himself up for good
in Albion

Only this I can say in full authority:
"To be safe in striking at the powerful
make sure that your blows are powerless."

V

No. I went down the road at night
walking
bubbling o'er with shouts and epithets
directed nowheres—
or was it up the road?

and listening
listening in the dark
in springtime

All seasons have their season
only if
each after its fashion ... only if
all seasons lead towards spring.

Listening while shouting in the springtime
while walking up and/or down the road—
my idiot Selphness

Oh, hear the frogpond in this selfsame season
how it totally anonymously yipes
each piper-upper in his particular way
a culmination of the endless past—unique.

Any and all of you
who somehow somewhere along the line
managed in some respect to prize-get
or like Shakespeare
who got no prize—
each of you unique
an idiot Selphness,
with satisfactions and disgruntlements its own only
while every eachness merges into allness

If but by definition,
the Law-Word loves us all
staying up all night to record each attitude
though usually refusing to give answer

All Names
and Namables
are but emergence
into ultimate Namelessness
an ideal consummate unitary Word for Everything—
the
Absolute

seeing every sunset/from every angle/at every instant,
and all the while
seeing every sunrise

AN ASSERTION TO END ON

Relaxing to the fall
hoarding accurate acute remembrances
pronouncing them beautiful
even as the body leans toward subsidence

saying thanks in principle
from amidst much bepuzzlement
a smile here, a caressing there
the click of an occasional expression

(for we are sentenced to the sentence)
and now, with the coming of spring
coming and coming and coming—
and the body (pause) . . .

This winter, having stayed north,
we earned the rights of spring—against snow
the chickadees learned to fly down
fly up and eat out of our hands

greedy wild frail bodies
their cold clutch on our fingers
they alighted and were proved right
in trusting us

Yes, by far (I guess)
the chance to have lived
outdoes
the need to die

LINES FROM OUT MY SCATTEREDHOOD

It was all there in First-Land
sweetly sleeping
peacefully infolded
the Primal Now all set to linger on
through Any-When
the moveless meaning beyond the verbal flux
the essence within existence
the Word within the words.

Oh, lead me to the First-Land
of Primal Any-When.

Word-logged, I praise
the Principle of Perfect Laudability
the Absolute Magistrate
(the Sanskrit HUTA, the Petitioned).

Drop the *a* (hence HUT)
change gutteral aitch to gutteral *g* (hence GUT)
make unvoiced *t* into its voiced cognate *d* (hence GUD)
allow for the minor ablaut transforming of *u* into *o*
—and Hail!
from the miracle potencies of speech
there stands forth
                    GOD
                            (revealed by logo-logic)

Oh, lead me to the First-Land
where all is sweet as dawn

birds singing in the mist in springtime
their avid taking-in and giving-forth
and me petitioning HUTA,
praising the Principle of Perfect Laudability.

Oh, lead me
to the dew
at dawn
in
First-
Land

Flowerishes

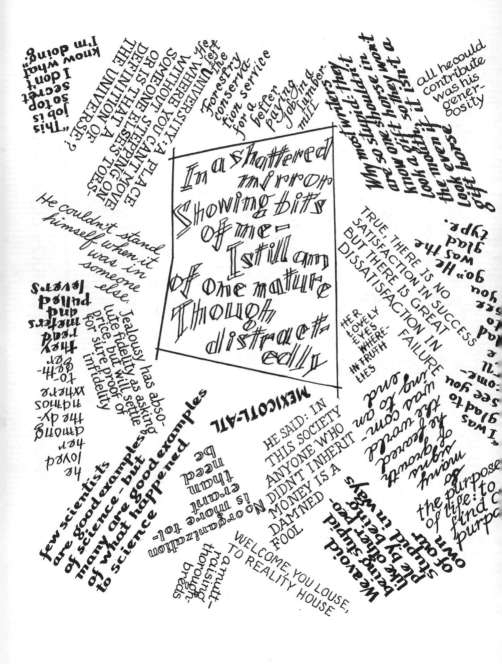

In a shattered mirror showing bits of me— I still am of one mature though distract-edly

"This job is so top secret I don't know what I'm doing."

THE UNIVERSE? OR IS THAT A PLACE WHERE YOU CAN'T MOVE WITHOUT STEPPING ON SOMEONE'S TOES. DEFINITELY THE

He left the University for a better paying job in the lumber mill. Forestry conservation for a service

My so-called motivators are you stupid that it surprises me? If you look at a gift horse, it isn't a how one who's a count.

all he could contribute was his generosity

Look closer the event gift type.

TRUE, THERE IS NO SATISFACTION IN SUCCESS BUT THERE IS GREAT SATISFACTION IN DISSATISFACTION — FAILURE

He couldn't stand himself when it was in someone else.

Jealousy has absolute fidelity as asking price, but will settle for sure proof of infidelity.

they read matters and pulled levers to-th-gat somewhere dy-among her loved he

HER LOVELY EYES WHERE-IN TRUTH LIES

was glad to "He was glad to see you go." to Pop — some-I'll see you

few scientists are good examples of science — but many are good examples of what happened to science

No organization is more tol-erant than they need be

MEXICOTL-ATL

HE SAID: IN THIS SOCIETY ANYONE WHO DIDN'T INHERIT MONEY IS A DAMNED FOOL

WELCOME YOU LOUSE, TO REALITY HOUSE

a multi-raising though-breeds

was working in the world. He found to ignore and to com-

I was glad to know of the purpose of life: to find a purpo

down to us Weavold Provide being their nee like their own in ways

IN THE DUSK
THE TALL CEDAR-
MEN STANDING
SO STILL

he was a lesbian interested in Ambi-guity both Sexual and Existential

ANIMALS ARE IDEAS WALKING IN THEIR SLEEP

TO COVER THEIR DE-LAY THEY TELL YOU TO HURRY

The task of a priest-hood: to sympathize with the lowly and side with the mighty.

FREEDOM IS THE STATE OF BEING ONE'S OWN SLAVEDRIVER

e raises ou con-fidentially s though t were a ecret

EVEN HUMILITY CAN GO TO ONE'S HEAD

MODERN IDEAL OF A HOME: A CROSS BETWEEN A STORE WINDOW AND HOSPITAL

Marriage is about to make people

ALTER ONE'S STARTING TERMS TO FIND OUT CONCLUSIONS

CRIME: next to defense, our biggest industry

BIRDS PEEPING AT THE PEEP OF DAY

It takes all kinds of worlds

he was her mentor, she his menturse

That special kind of hate: APARTHEID

NOT THAT I HAVE BEEN DIFFERENT BUT ONLY THAT I AM IN WAYS OF BEING WHAT HAD BEEN MORE PRIMITIVE WISHING

At college try to get things straight— You'll have all the rest of your life to get them crooked

hanging at the crossroads

a boomerang

A soft-spoken cross-burning self-righteier

The JEW offered $6 but the GENTILE goyed him up to ten

CULTURE LOVE- LIEST OF TAX DODGES

"ECHO" he shouted— and Echo answered— "E GO"

transforming chaos into ordure

Horrified over population and pollution, he popularized problems of contraindrums

Poets with little to say learn to write as though guarding a secret

ARE POEMS PSYCHANDA?

HE WAS AST OUT

WAITING WITH DOG EYES TO BE SHOWN THE DOOR

WANTED: a non- habit- forming habit

ALL WE NEED FEAR IS LACK OF FEAR ITSELF

bacteriological Laboratory hits the Twister when the day from us Godsave

RUSTY WITH IRONY

FIELDS LYING SILENT IN THE SONGFUL DAWN

They would fight dirty wars with clean bombs?

WHEN THE GLACIERS COME, push- ing pieces of The Merritt Parkway into South Carolina